Generation Wealth

How Young Adults Can Build a Fortune, Retire
Early, and Navigate Cryptocurrencies

Jacob Reed

Contents

1.

2.

3.

4.

5.

6.

7.

Introduction

You must be on fire! You have long yearned not to work by the clock in exchange for a 401(k) plan in your old age. Your life is now! Will you let your best days pass by doing tasks that nowadays can be easily replaced by a machine and surrounding yourself with a low value lifestyle? Clearly not.

Retiring early is a big dream, one of freedom, less stress, and more agency. For instance, if your dream is jet skiing, but you decide to postpone it until retirement, will you enjoy it more at 30, 45, or 65? But this is not just about enjoying life better; it's about getting away from work toxicity. We live in a world where loneliness and agency are continually avoided, but these two work as reminders for you to take more quality time for yourself. This higher quality is what enables a higher sense of fulfillment. And you'll wait until when? When your body no longer answers you and your time is spent in health care facility waiting rooms?

I also know that wealth matters to you; this is the main tenet of early retirement. Most examples of early retirement work from a hyper-saving, expenditure cutting approach to devote as much money as possible into investing. If your income is median, i.e., below six figures yearly, you'll find this a bit hard at first, especially as financial freedom comes from early investment, which requires saving. But here comes a new asset class to the rescue, one that can take you from micro-investing to the big leagues: cryptocurrency.

While still unknown to many, the cryptocurrency market is one that is ripe with opportunity. Bitcoin, the most famous currency in

1

the market, has increased its value by 5,488.11% over the last seven years (Buy Bitcoin Worldwide, 2023). This makes it a promising market for increasing one's wealth, provided that it's backed up with the best investment strategy. It also makes it one of the markets that'll help you retire earlier, even with a median income.

So I'll be helping you retire early by focusing on cryptocurrencies. But this isn't a crypto course alone. Randomly treating an asset such as crypto can be a bad idea, so I'll take you step by step through a proper use of crypto currency for an early retirement. The first step, then, is learning to invest. I'll give you the fundamentals of investing so you can start on the right foot.

I know that you are aiming, consciously or unconsciously, towards an early retirement. But a big goal doesn't come true without thorough planning. Here is where we start, with our feet on the ground but our eyes in the sky. Planned investment will boost your chances of an earlier retirement by aiming to grow from reality rather than fantasy.

Once we've built a solid foundation with the right investing mentality, we'll start applying these techniques to cryptocurrencies. We'll start by gaining insight into cryptocurrencies and their supporting technology, the blockchain, as an asset, and the market risks and opportunities it presents. Then, we'll close by developing a solid investment strategy based on crypto. Are you into Generation Wealth?

Chapter 1: Building Wealth—Investing Fundamentals for Young Adults

Generation Wealth is your generation, one where building wealth is within reach for everyone willing to make the effort. With wealth comes the opportunity for early retirement from toxic work. Yet building wealth has some basic concepts you need to start managing before you can actually start changing your current reality.

Let's start with interest and a powerful aspect to it: compounding.

The Power of Compound Interest

To take advantage of compound interest, you simply reinvest interest as capital, allowing you to increase your capabilities of earning interest. This simple trick that allows you to get rich can also be used against you to make you poor. There are two basic parties interested in your poverty, beyond the occasional scammer, who will accept your becoming impoverished to protect their interests:

1. **The State**: It will compound against you through inflation to meet monetary and fiscal policy goals.
2. **Creditors**: They will compound against you for any unpaid capital and interest to protect their credits.

From this basic explanation, we can extrapolate three conclusions:

1. Outstanding debt will make you poorer.
2. Inflation will make you poorer.
3. Compounding interest from investments will make you richer.

So, a first formula for wealth would be:

Compound interest $>$ Purchasing power lost $+$ Outstanding debt

In a nutshell, what we are aiming for is to earn more through investment than we lose in purchasing power through inflation and interest on debt. As soon as you understand this and start hedging against these risks, you'll stop losing key value for your early retirement. Don't let inflation and debt take away your precious time, either!

Beyond this, there are two other key aspects to compounding that create a snowball effect in wealth building: frequency and time. Compounding is not a one-off strategy but a strategy for life. You always suffer from inflation, and you always enter into debts—why not make investment an eternal endeavor? But investing for life will not cut it alone. You need frequency for compounding to work its magic. The more times you compound, the bigger the margin you'll obtain from your initial investment. I won't ask you to believe me or give you fancy numbers. Just check any compound interest calculator online and do the math. Your agency toward compounding starts now.

Different Types of Investments

So, now that we understand that wealth is created by investment and multiplied by reinvesting, let's take a look at the different kinds of investments you can make:

1. **Lending:** By lending, you can earn capital plus interest. The most basic forms of lending are CDs in banks, and DeFi lending in the crypto market.

2. **Contributing:** By contribution, you can ask back dividends in exchange for your initial investment. The most basic forms of

contributions are investments into businesses, stocks, trusts, funds, annuities, REITs and contribution plans.

3. **Leasing:** By providing something you own for a period of time, you can earn rent until it fulfills its use. This would mainly happen with immovables and cars.

4. **Reselling:** The idea of resale is basic: Buy low and sell high. Real estate and commodities, including cryptocurrencies, are some options within our interests.

Whenever you are on the client side of any of these operations, you aren't investing but rather spending or saving. For instance, when you buy a home, you pay both the purchase price and mortgage interest. You aren't investing in real estate yet, unless you lease or resell the property you bought. This means that in finances, goods can work like assets (income generating goods) or liabilities (expenditure generating goods). Coming back to the house, you might be buying it to save on future rent or land costs. But until you put that house under a mortgage, you'll have a big liability in your life that you'll have to account for as a possible stumbling block for your early retirement.

Risk and Return

Now that we know that we need to raise money from investments and which activities are investments, we can work on the two ends of any investment, risk, i.e., what you stand to lose, and return, i.e. what you stand to win. There's generally a rule in investing that the higher the risk you take, the higher the reward you may obtain, but that's a double-edged sword that can be quite stingy for the inexperienced investor.

But with risk aversion in mind, several investment profiles have been created. Think of these profiles as a spectrum, and you can stand anywhere in these profiles, but you are most likely to start as a conservative investor, become a moderate one, and then end as an aggressive one. But there might be many barriers to adding aggressiveness to your investment; therefore, compounding is necessary to accelerate the benefits of a low-risk, low-reward approach to investment.

So let's look at the three models:

1. **Conservative:** A conservative profile just seeks to beat inflation, but it doesn't necessarily aim to beat the market or follow it. Generally, a conservative investor will avoid risky investments, but some shares and commodities may be acquired as part of the strategy. The key goal here is to protect cash flow.

2. **Moderate:** A moderate profile seeks portfolio appreciation, i.e., to have investments rise in their value while keeping their investments stabilized. The goal here shifts from protecting cash flow to building wealth. A moderate investor will aim for diversification and hedging against risks, so as to obtain moderate gains from a bull market and minimum losses from a bear market.

3. **Aggressive:** An aggressive profile will seek long-term gains and stomach any kind of volatility, including possible big slumps in portfolio value, with the hopes of earning more money by beating the market in a long span of time, like ten years or more. Generally, this profile requires some expertise,

which I assume you still don't have. Prepare yourself for this type of investment, but don't overdo it until you've gained solid experience as an investor.

Starting off as a conservative investor isn't a bad thing, especially if you suffer negative cash flow, i.e., not having cash available when you need it. Eventually, you'll have to increase aggressiveness in your investments. Otherwise, you are quite likely to get stuck in your status quo, which will harm your potential to retire earlier.

Now, neither aggressive nor conservative are profiles for life. There are different moments in life: one for increasing value, one for consolidating value, and one for turning value into income. If you understand the analogy, then you know that you'll be going through the three profiles at different moments of your life.

Then, if you are going into trading, you need to keep in mind the risk-reward ratio. I'll be asking you to apply a stop loss at 2% and an exit price at 6%, and you may ask yourself, "Why these numbers? Why should I aim to lose only two percent and only earn 6%?" While these numbers are intentionally low for risk management purposes, they follow a logic: They are in the ideal risk-reward ratio, a 1:3 ratio, where for every loss, you stand to win at least three times. And if you do the math, you'll know that 2:6 = 1:3. Of course, as you get more proficient at assessing risks and rewards, you may try more challenging ratios.

How to Create a Diversified Investment Portfolio

You need to understand that while we'll be focusing on crypto, just one asset won't help you meet your goals. Also, most investor profiles consider three kinds of investment: bonds, cash (money market and CDs), and stock investment. There's more to that than just these three investments; you have funds and indexes following these investments, real estate, and commodities, which include cryptocurrency.

Diversification is an income stream multiplication technique. If you just work from 9 a.m. to 6 p.m. and that's it, you have a single income stream. If you lose your job, you'll have zero income streams and zero cash flow, and you are broke. Diversification is about hedging against losing income streams. Two jobs can be two income streams, but then there's so little time available for regular work. So, you need assets to work for you as well; that's the concept behind making investments. Diversification is just having different sorts of assets work for you in tandem, so that if one goes down, the others keep feeding you. This is wealth 101.

This diversity can come in two ways: having assets of a different kind or holding assets of a similar kind. For instance, gold, wheat, and cryptocurrencies are assets of a similar kind, as they are all commodities and operate similarly, but their nature and risk are different. The same goes for stocks and bonds. There are different companies, states, and industries. But you need to know that most times you'll start small, so your best option for stocks, bonds, and certain commodities can be an exchange fund, where you own a portion of a pool of diversified assets.

When investing in different sectors and instruments, the best advice we can take home is to invest in things we know and understand with as much diversity as possible, within manageable possibilities. A manageable portfolio would consider up to 30 instruments or vehicles, no more. Some of these vehicles should be funds, which secure further diversification. With diversification, it's best to invest regularly and sell off whatever asset may be perceived as losing value within a five-year period.

So, how should we diversify? First, consider your available cash, for that will determine what your initial investment can be, and then follow this pattern: (1) hedging against negative cash flow; (2) having an emergency fund; and (3) increasing the value of a portfolio. You can't be wealthy without money, and you can't ensure the availability of money if you don't save for a rainy day. Once you have that cleared up, you can then start growing.

Once you have the money to invest, you should consider complementary instruments or industries. Consider a videoconferencing stock and a delivery stock. As these two activities are unrelated, the stocks, as high-risk assets, see their risks lowered when considered as a portfolio, since a crisis in the videoconferencing market will not affect the delivery market whatsoever. You may also consider market capitalization or size for diversifying equity, and credit quality for diversifying debt instruments.

Furthermore, having the money to invest is closely linked to your monetary needs now. The more money you need now, the more liquid your investments should be. And this is tricky because, generally, it's the least liquid assets that raise the most value. Liquid assets generally provide income rather than value. And cryptocurrencies, which can also be used as a store-for-value despite being liquid assets, take full market cycles to increase in value, which in crypto markets is around four years and in stock markets, seven.

Next, you should diversify, considering time and risk aversion as well. You'll need money for purchases, so investing should be goal oriented. If you need money to make a purchase, you'll need some time to liquidate your investment. So, the recommendation is this: The sooner you'll need the money, the less risk you should take.

Let's consider some kinds of assets to see their pros and cons. I'll save cryptocurrencies for later, but consider them as assets sharing the characteristics of fiat money and commodities.

1. **Fiat money/cash:** Fiat money, legal tender, or cash are all just plain money as approved by Central Banks. There are a few investments you can make with them like currency arbitrage, lending, and depositing, but you'll be using it mainly for cash reserves and emergency funds.

   a. **Pros:** Having sufficient cash allows you to face your needs now.

   b. **Cons:** If not properly invested, it can lose value to inflation. Hence, money either needs to be saved with interest, invested, or spent within a month of collection.

   c. **Risk:** Low to moderate. It increases with stringent and unreliable monetary policy.

2. **Debt Instruments:** Mainly bonds, this is money you lend in exchange for interest. In debt instruments, you may collect interests regularly or upon maturity date, and these may also be fixed or variable. Generally, the risk associated with debt is that of the debtors' creditworthiness. The higher the creditworthiness, the lower the risk. This risk can be further

lowered by collateralizing or extending privilege status for liquidation.

   a. **Pros:** It's a low-risk instrument ideal for compounding strategies.

   b. **Cons:** You depend on the creditor's willingness to pay, and you may need to sell or discount the instrument to liquidate it if you can't wait until the maturity date. This may cause you to lose capital or interest, but it's also a good strategy for stopping losses.

   c. **Risk:** Low to moderate. Risks may be hedged through collateral, privileges, or balancing.

3. **Equity Instruments:** These are rights to participate politically or economically in a given corporation or venture. Equity instruments have variable rents. Their price is volatile and economic rights may not always result in the distribution of dividends.

   a. **Pros:** These instruments are adequate for portfolio valuation, and are easy to liquidate unless the sale of equity requires approval by management and other equity holders.

   b. **Cons:** Direct investment in equity requires solid market and business study. If you don't understand the business or don't have enough capital to invest, it might not be an adequate option for you.

   c. **Risk:** High. To moderate risk, it requires cash as a backup, stop-losses, and diversification.

4. **Certificates of Deposit (CDs):** These are loans to financial entities bearing interest that is collected upon maturity.

    a. **Pros:** It's an instrument ideal for compounding and building retirement reserves.

    b. **Cons:** You need to wait upon maturity to collect both capital and interest, which may be troublesome if you have cash shortages.

    c. **Risk:** Low. Make sure to maintain a healthy cash flow when investing in them.

5. **Money Market:** These are interest-bearing accounts or funds which may place limits on withdrawal rights, but don't freeze money like CDs.

    a. **Pros:** It provides competitive interest that's ideal for setting up emergency funds, since money is generally available at the moment or within 48 hours max.

    b. **Cons:** It will lose value in an inflationary environment.

    c. **Risk:** Low. Use dollar-cost averaging to compound them.

6. **Funds:** These are collections of equity or debt instruments, where you hold a part of the fund. The fund manager may choose to reinvest or distribute dividends.

    a. **Pros:** It's an ideal instrument for diversification and small investments. Plus, it's easy to liquidate.

    b. **Cons:** You depend on the manager's prowess to keep the fund's yield profitable over time. You may have to do fee shopping to find the right fund.

c. **Risk:** Low to high. Funds that are pegged to indexes are generally the ones to enjoy more longevity.

7. **Trusts:** These are agreements whereby investors may participate as beneficiaries of a venture managed by a trustee. They can provide both variable and fixed rent, and property rights as well.

   a. **Pros:** Ideal for investing in retailers, wholesalers, and real estate when your cash isn't enough to invest directly in them.

   b. **Cons:** You depend on the trustee's expertise, and unless certificates of debt or participation have gone through an Initial Public Offering, they are quite hard to sell.

   c. **Risk:** Moderate to high. Balance with low-risk instruments.

8. **Real Estate:** This is simply land. You can buy it for sale or lease, or you may lease as a sublease.

   a. **Pros:** It's an increasingly scarce asset, so its valuation is ever-rising.

   b. **Cons:** Land can be trespassed upon, and litigation costs tend to be high. You may face high maintenance costs. Also, it's a highly illiquid asset.

   c. **Risk:** Moderate to high. Balance with low-risk instruments. Avoid selling when there are bear markets with liquidity crises. That's the ideal moment for buying.

9. **Movables:** These include vehicles, furniture, or any other property right that can be moved but cannot be consumed nor is fungible (interchangeable by one of the same kind).

   a. **Pros:** These can increase in value through improvements. In addition, they hold value better than fiat money.

   b. **Cons:** Amortization, obsolescence, and maintenance costs may cause you to lose your spread on the sale.

   c. **Risk:** Moderate. Consider insurance.

10. **Commodities:** These are either fungible or consumables that can be stockpiled or used as production inputs.

   a. **Pros:** Their market value tends to be asynchronous, in that they don't depend on stock or bonds, and rarely do they relate with each other, as with gold and food. Hence, it's ideal for hedging against equity.

   b. **Cons:** Storage costs should be considered.

   c. **Risk:** Moderate to high. Consider insurance.

11. **Intellectual Property:** These are property rights over the act of creating art, brands, and inventions. It needs to be original and registered for it to be valuable.

   a. **Pros:** These rights can be sold, leased, or attached, and you can obtain income through royalty.

   b. **Cons:** It's a win-lose game. If your creation doesn't affect people's lives, you'll bear a 100% loss.

   c. **Risk:** Moderate. You need considerable legal protection to make money out of it.

12. **Art**: These are actual pieces of art, detached from their property rights, and held as a collection.

   a. **Pros:** These become valuable over time, especially if the work contributes significantly to the art scene. Plus, the crypto market has found ways of amplifying investments in works of art.

   b. **Cons:** There can be strange bubbles, and conservation costs are high.

   c. **Risk:** High. Consider insurance, and protect yourself against counterfeits.

Getting acquainted with the risk of these assets matters, as the key to any portfolio involves: (a) securing revenue, (b) increasing and stabilizing value, (c) multiplying income streams, and (d) minimizing risks. But before you can do anything with your portfolio, you should consider setting your investment goals.

Importance of Setting Investment Goals

You don't need money for money's sake. In itself, money has no value. What has value are the things you can purchase with it. So the question you'd have to ask yourself is, "What would I need to purchase now, in a few years, and in my retirement?" These would be your goals in the short, mid, and long term.

We know that retiring early is a long-term goal, so we need to focus on getting ready as soon as possible for aggressive investing. So, the preconditions for a long-term investment should be satiating any cash flow problems and getting an emergency fund operational.

Once those conditions are in place, an investment goal needs to have these components:

1. **Initial capital:** This is the amount of money you are willing to invest.
2. **Time for contribution:** How long it'll take you to invest it.
3. **Risk:** This will decide the kind of asset you'll be investing in.
4. **Money goal:** This is the amount of money you desire to raise after investment.
5. **Date for completion:** This will set the time by which you should meet your goal.
6. **Need:** This is the need that the investment will satisfy.

   With these, you can make yourself accountable for the goals you set. You shouldn't set stringent or lax goals. Remember that if you use compounding, your investment capabilities will increase over time, so goals need to be revised and readjusted as you progress in your investment endeavors. Don't rest on your laurels.

Strategies for Achieving Investment Goals

Many roads lead to Rome, but each road has its shortcuts . Here are some strategies by which you can use for increasing the value of your portfolio:

1. **Retirement accounts:** Many invest in IRA plans, like the 401(k). The issue is that this strategy isn't necessarily the best for early retirement, as they are meant to be collected by a given age, generally 60 years old. This strategy is complementary in that it can provide a stream at an older age, where maintaining income streams may be harder due to health issues.
2. **Buy-and-hold:** To buy and hold is to buy a given amount of an asset, and resell it some years later when the value has

increased considerably over time. Again, this is good for risky, long-term strategies.

3. **Momentum investing:** Here the idea is to buy at a low price, an entry price, and sell at a higher price, the exit price. This pattern of selling and reselling is short or mid term. This strategy is solid for compounding.

4. **Dollar-cost averaging:** Instead of looking for an entry or exit price, this method allows you to purchase an asset at an average value, which will even the risk out by consistently entering at regular time intervals for a given asset. This is a risk-hedging strategy, and one that's easy to automate, especially if you invest in cryptocurrency.

5. **Index investing:** To invest in an index or a fund is to gain access to an already diversified portfolio in the form of a share. Given that these indexes are managed, they have costs that may require shopping (i.e., looking for the cheapest fund).

6. **Growth investing**: The key here lies in studying the market for stocks or commodities that show potential for growth in the near future. This strategy is risky, as most of the businesses that fall into this category are startups.

7. **Value investing:** Investing in value means looking for undervalued stocks or commodities in comparison with their actual performance in the primary market. This strategy allows you to hedge against beat-or-bust startups.

8. **Income investing:** This is using fixed-rent assets, dividend stocks, rent, or DeFi interest for compounding the interest you earn on them. This kind of investment is used to set multiple income streams that pay off at regular intervals.

9. **Arbitrage:** It's a buying and selling, or leasing and subleasing technique where a margin is obtained by offering an asset in a market different to that where it was purchased. This technique can be used in currencies, the exchange markets, and most notably, rent.

In the crypto market, the most used strategies are buy-and-hold, momentum investing, dollar-cost averaging, and income investing. The other strategies are a bit hard to use in the crypto market, though value investing could be used with Ethereum due to the nature of its virtual reality machine. I'll discuss in greater detail later.

Day Trading

Before we move on, let's talk a bit about the elements of momentum investing, a.k.a. Day Trading. In day trading, you should have certain elements in place:

1. **Entry price:** Price at which you buy the asset. You generally enter when the asset price curve is rising.

2. **Exit price:** The price at which you sell the asset to earn a spread. Generally set at 6% above the entry price.

3. **Stop loss:** The price at which you sell the asset to prevent a loss. Generally set at 2% below the entry price.

While there are other techniques to set an exit price and a stop loss, these two numbers are the easiest for beginners. You can research those techniques later on. The idea behind this is calculated risk: you buy when there's a chance for the price to rise, you set an exit price to ensure a profit, and you set a stop loss to prevent losses you can't cover with your cash reserves. Leaving a stock for too long under momentum trading is simply too risky. If your idea is to hold, then don't consider day trading; instead, look for the asset you've bought in a month or so. Now, remember that day trading is a risky strategy with a risky asset. This means you'll need an investment plan telling you how much you can put into your trading strategy.

As you move on, you'll want to know the right time to buy a stock. While you shouldn't aim to beat the market, there are four indicators for buying and selling:

1. **Support:** This is a bottom price level of the asset, indicating a good buying price.
2. **Resistance:** This is a peak price level of the asset, indicating a good selling price.
3. **Long:** This is a position where you believe that the asset will appreciate as the asset has hit support, hence you buy.
4. **Short:** This is a position where you believe that the asset will depreciate as the asset has hit resistance, hence you sell.

With these values, you can see an entry pattern when an asset hits support and then rises, and an exit pattern when the asset hits resistance and then dips. What matters here is not beating the market but yourself. You'll face many losses and many wins, but if your stop orders are carefully set and you follow them, you are set to win on average more than you lose.

Chapter 2: Retiring Early—Planning for Financial Independence

So far, we have been dealing with some basic investing principles, but as I stated before, you aren't investing randomly but with views on early retirement. Now, the earlier you retire, the more expenses you'll need to cover. So, that's something to keep in mind. You can't hope to retire with only a median income. We need to grow that money. So let's discuss how much money you require to wave bye bye to toxic work.

How Much Money Do You Need to Retire Early?

Let's not talk about a given amount of money, but about proportions. Lifestyle and needs determine the amount of money you need, including for inflation. Even if inflation is low, you need to account for it. A dollar today will be worth more than a dollar tomorrow. That's the sad reality of our economy worldwide. Now, there's a definite cost to our lifestyle—we only need to calculate it, and for that, we need a budget. Also, you have a life expectancy—if unsure, set it to 82—and a desired retirement age, which will produce the amount of time you'll be retired. With these three key indicators, we can come up with a simple formula for retirement:

Retirement funds = Average yearly expenditure * years in retirement * inflation rate

Then, after calculating your retirement amount, check how far away you are from that goal. Simply pick your budget and check your disposable income—the money you have to spare after making all your expenditures. That's the money you now have available for investing, unless you commit yourself to a given strategy, forego expenditures, pay off debt, and set up an emergency fund.

But the key here is your withdrawal rate—how much money you'll actually be withdrawing per month. The earlier you retire, the lower the withdrawal rate. Generally, withdrawals peak at 4% with a retirement age of 65. From there, the retirement rate goes downward. With this number, you can find the goal easier:

Retirement funds = Average yearly expenditure * 100 / withdrawal rate

This second equation is far easier than the first one, but it requires consistency in your withdrawals once you start collecting. The idea is that every year you save a portion of the amount you'll need to retire. Therefore, there's another way to calculate this:

Retirement date = Your age + (Retirement / Average yearly expenditure)

However, there's a caveat to this. Generally, people tend to save more as they grow older. So, this calculation may give you the average, but not the exact time of your retirement. Anyways, you can find calculators online for early retirement if you want to do things faster. I'm providing you with the calculus so you can think things through.

Strategies for Achieving Financial Independence

Approaches to retirement can be fast, slow, or stepped. You can save hard and fast, and you could retire as soon as possible. You may also save at a slower rate yet aim for retirement age earlier than 65. Finally, with a stepped approach, you downgrade your full-time job into a part-time job and save at the rate that the part-time job affords you, while enjoying a partial retirement now.

Now your retirement goals can always be met from two main paths: an increase in income streams or a decrease in expenditure. You can blend these two together to your own taste to make your perfect retirement mix. But, remember, you will always have to reach a retirement goal in a given amount of time.

Then, there are other aspects of financial independence to turn our attention to:

1. **Lifestyle creep:** When income streams increase, so does spending. It's natural for us to spend more if we earn more. However, this doesn't have to affect saving goals. So being able to fast from spending is a key skill to develop for our financial independence endeavors.

2. **Accountability:** We've discussed budgeting as key for pinpointing the retirement age. But the true reason behind budgeting is holding yourself accountable. You'll find it hard to save if you don't control your finances adequately.

3. **Family support:** If you live in a family, then you know they all work as a unit. Or at least they are supposed to. If there's any toxic approach to money, you need to detoxify it. And sometimes this might be impossible, to the point of leading to breakups. Other times, retiring early isn't in your partner's mind. So, you'll be alone in your path. But what matters the most is the will to keep your retirement endeavors ongoing even if you need to make compromises from time to time to keep your family united.

4. **Panic purchases and sales:** Panic is the worst feeling in relation to finances. You stand to lose a lot if you buy and sell in a panic. Buying in panic causes an artificial increase in any input to your life that may deregulate your budget. A funny example of this would be the toilet paper shortage during pandemics. But also, selling under panic is bad, as your exit price will surely be lower than your entry price, and you'll be losing money. If the exit price is low, the best strategy is to hold.

5. **Purchases on sale:** Being mindful of prices in the market and having a spending cushion matter to get good deals that'll save you money in the near future or the long term. For instance, buying property while in a recession is a good move, as you'll be entering at a price below the market average.

6. **Balanced savings:** In counterpoint to lifestyle creep, an excess of frugality may lead you to a miser's life. You'll want to avoid assuming voluntary poverty outside a legitimate religious practice that gives meaning to your underconsumption. After all, you live in the world and you should be enjoying it.

7. **Having a purpose:** There's something you may wish now, but are resigning to, in order to make it to the next day. This desire must be at the heart of your retirement. If you retire without meaning, you'll be yearning to go back to work in order to fill the meaninglessness in your life.

With lifestyle creep and slips in mind, it's key to start budgeting to keep track of yourself. Think of your budget as a journal for the first leg of your retirement plan: having a consistent spending rate that enables you to save better. If your retirement plan includes actually inflating your lifestyle, then you need to account for it as a bigger retirement number and also plan the best sequence for inflating your lifestyle. Doing it all at once might be too risky for you.

Then, work around your habits in both savings and relationships. Saving for retirement should be a seamless experience. If you still find it hard, you should try out automated savings. Also, keep your lifestyle and your social circle as aligned with your retirement goal as possible. Keeping with the Joneses is a powerful bias, and the best way to leverage it is to have friends who share a similar lifestyle to that you dream of.

With these tips in mind, you can move forward with your financial independence strategy. Remember to never lose sight of your retirement goals and to keep grinding on your saving and investment endeavors.

Building a Retirement Portfolio

We've been hinting about a portfolio, but we haven't stopped to consider the details behind its creation, so there are three key aspects to building portfolios:

1. **Cash reserve:** A cash reserve means having a year of your budget in cash or highly liquid instruments, like money market accounts. If you want to make your cash reserve resilient to economic downturns, you'll need two to four years of your budget in easy-to-liquidate instruments, like certificates of deposit. This reserve is not for emergencies, but

for protecting your portfolio's value and keeping your lifestyle stable.

2. **Emergency funds:** The idea of an emergency fund is to build up a reserve for emergencies without affecting your retirement portfolio. These emergencies fall in the category of unexpected expenses, like illnesses and repairs, and possible risks while the retirement fund is built up, like being unemployed. The best place for an emergency fund is a savings account, as these accounts tend to punish excessive withdrawals. The ideal amount to be saved is a year and a half of your income.

3. **Strategy shifting:** There are three stages of your portfolio's life: (1) income generation before retirement, (2) consolidation, and (3) income generation post retirement. If you recall our discussion on investor profiles, you'd realize that a conservative strategy focuses on income, while an aggressive strategy focuses on wealth. At the start of your investing life, you simply lack the income to build wealth—that's why you're likely to play a conservative game. But as your income streams become stable, you can increase aggressiveness in your investing, so that you can build wealth adequately for the time you retire. Now, once you are retired, you are likely to gradually fall back into a conservative strategy again to compensate for the loss of your job as an income stream, and increased spending with the passing of time.

As I have mentioned before, any portfolio has two preconditions: proper cash flow and an emergency fund to back it up. From there on, building a portfolio becomes easy, especially if you use compounding the right way.

Importance of Asset Allocation

As you build your portfolio, you'll be managing different kinds of assets. The proportion of each asset you hold with respect to your portfolio is known as asset allocation. Remember, again, that asset here includes only the income-generating property. Financially speaking, consumption goods and immovables are liabilities. The idea behind allocation is to find a balance between income generation and wealth building, with each asset covering the risks of the other.

The other key to asset allocation is your aversion to risk, which determines your investor profile. While you want to increase your aggressiveness as you solidify your income streams, there's a limit to the amount of risk you can possibly withstand before you enter panic selling and lose any value you wish to amass. So you need to be self-aware of your fears and investment patterns.

So, let's take yet another look at the three main investors' profiles, this time focusing on allocation:

1. **Conservative:** In a conservative portfolio, you'll have a small portion of stock or equities, generally 20%, and no more. These stocks are quite likely to include blue-chip companies only. Then, another 40% may reside in exchange-traded funds or mutual funds, where risk is pooled by a professional investor. 20% may stay in bonds, especially those with low yield and risk. ETFs and mutual funds take up a higher portion of the portfolio because these instruments have the

benefit of providing both low risk and high diversification. This portfolio can increase in aggressiveness if 5% of the bonds moves to commodities like gold and art, while shifting up to 20% from ETFs to equity. Bonds can easily be replaced by interest-yielding stablecoins.

2. **Moderate:** With a moderate portfolio, you will shift from blue-chip stocks into growth investing, which will present 50% of your portfolio. Here, you'll be aiming to increase your portfolio value rather than increasing your income. Next would be the use of cryptocurrency as commodities for up to 10% of your portfolio. This would include the two main coins only, Bitcoin and Ethereum. Then, your ETFs or funds will take 20%, but you'll be focusing on diversifying them by sector or industry to cover against potential risks. The rest of your portfolio will be shared by REITs, bonds, commodities, and other investments.

3. **Aggressive:** An aggressive portfolio concentrates on big returns over stable income. It starts with equity, with a 60% allocation. These stocks can be from anywhere in the world, the key is to do both growth and value investment. Then, the cryptocurrency allocation increases to 15%, to include altcoins in your investments. Then 10% of your investments should be shifting to real estate, which should stabilize your portfolio with a steady income. The remainder may be invested in commodities, funds, alternative investments, and equity crowdfunding. Aggressiveness may be reinforced by increasing the crypto allocation to 25% and shifting equity crowdfunding to 10%.

These examples of allocation are meant to give you a picture of what a portfolio may look like for any of the investor profiles, yet they are models. It's up to you to find the right blend of assets to allocate as you live up to your retirement goals. Remember that once you are nearing your retirement goal, you should be downscaling to more conservative investments so you can secure the value you have already amassed through your efforts.

Then there's the reality that all of this may still be confusing to you, and you don't know where to start. In such a case, there are always investors willing to share their allocation and explain the basics of it to you, and you may follow that investor and his allocation strategy. This is known as copy-trading. It has the downside of copying a person with a strategy that doesn't necessarily fit your current situation, but it'll simplify your investment choices and steer you clear of lousy investment advice.

Tax Considerations for Retirement Accounts

The key consideration in any retirement account are pre-tax (IRA) and after-tax (Roth IRA) accounts, meaning whether you wish to pay taxes as you withdraw (pre-tax) or as you contribute (after-tax). Being able to weigh the pros and cons of both types of retirement accounts will help you make the best of both worlds.

What is key in taxation are income brackets—the higher your income, the more taxes you'll be expected to pay. So, an advantage of pre-tax is that the income brackets of the retired are lower than those of the active population. However, the after-tax account allows you to accrue interest without taxation after you meet the qualification criteria, which generally involves holding the money until a certain age. In a pre-tax account, your interest will be taxed as well. So, this data is key for early retirement.

It's possible to blend both IRAs and Roth IRAs, so you can have an account where you may withdraw money before the statutory retirement age by paying taxes once you withdraw (IRA) and another account where you pay taxes only on capital contributions and withdraw tax-free once you reach the statutory retirement age (Roth IRA). Think of this as a sort of tax hedging. Though you'll want to get counsel from an accountant to make the best mix of IRAs and Roth IRAs.

Strategies for Managing Retirement Risks

Let's see some retirement risks and how we can prevent and face them:

1. **Longevity and frailty**: We save with the number 82 in mind. It's not conscious, but it's as high a life expectancy as we can generally hope for. We know we'll die some day, hopefully in our eighties, and this is embedded in some investments, especially annuities. But if we outlive our expectations, we may run out of funds. Then, there's the reality that at a certain age we lose our swing. We need to be able to teach or pay someone to assist us with financial management in our old age and hope that our trustee doesn't abuse us. Here's one of the reasons why the proper upbringing of your children matters.

2. **Inflation:** We need to understand that inflation is something to be concerned about. We need to know that inflation significantly decreases our capabilities of withdrawing, and may force us to keep growing our portfolio even beyond

retirement. We need to learn to adjust our savings and investments by inflation to see whether we are in a winning or losing game. The easiest thing to do is to use a relatively stable good as a comparative, to check whether we are on a winning or losing streak. You will also want to have investments where you can transfer the cost of inflation to other people, like dividend stocks or real estate rent.

3. **Excess withdrawal:** We need to come back to our retirement formula and understand that a 10% withdrawal rate is outright dangerous—this is far too high. Moreover, you need to check that your withdrawal isn't significantly affecting your capabilities of accruing further interest without decapitalizing.

4. **Health care:** We'll all face health issues sooner than later. Now, there's a basic principle: we should be able to pay health care insurance, from as young as possible. That's why getting as many income streams as possible matters. When we face a health issue we need to check whether the health issue is acute or chronic. An acute problem is generally faced with an emergency fund; whereas, a chronic illness needs to be considered in your budget as an ordinary expense, and you need to build up sufficient cash reserves to face it.

5. **Market risk:** A retirement strategy means that we'll be raising a portfolio, the value of which depends both on our decisions and market trends. It's not the same to retire in a bull market as a bear market. We've already discussed having backup cash reserves in semi-liquid instruments for a term of two to four years of your annual spending. Then, there's the reality that income from a portfolio isn't fixed but variable, so

you need to account for that in your withdrawals so you don't go beyond your withdrawal rate.

6. **Forced retirement:** The reality for many is that our jobs are still our main source of income, and hence we are unable to retire now. So if we're on unemployment or out of work due to an occupational or personal hazard, there'll be a time when we can't work, and this time can stretch from days to our whole life. If it's just a few days or even a year, we have our cash reserves and emergency fund to consume before digging into our portfolio. But insurance matters: workers', unemployment, and personal insurance should be here to cover this risk.

7. **Family:** Family challenges are also very important to manage. You must consider both internal and external risks. Raising your children the right way and managing any toxic elements of your family unit are the two main hedges against internal risks. Then, caring for kids now or later on is a challenge that'll require you to increase both your cash reserves and emergency fund before resuming any grinding on growing your portfolio. The same goes for losing a spouse. Your spouse may account for part or all of your income, so that's a big risk to hedge against. If you never managed money on your own or if you lag behind your spouse, start to raise money for your retirement now. Also, a spouse is a great emotional support. You need to get ready for the time you'll be alone.

8. **Public policy:** The State is a bigger player than we account for. A bad macro policy has a butterfly effect on the micro.

Our investments can rise or fall due to policy, which means that the investor who wishes to retire early must learn the art of flexibility and creativity. Otherwise, you'll lose your retirement dreams to comply with ill-made public policy.

Generally, the best way of hedging against many of the retirement risks is to actually build up our portfolio diligently. But even diligence may not suffice. Here's where insurance comes in to cover some of these costs. We need to build up our income streams so we can afford insurance that may cover risks. But above all things, take care of your family, and keep it free from harm from both within and without.

Now that we've got covered the basics of overall investing, let's consider the novel investing opportunity of cryptocurrencies.

Chapter 3: Navigating Cryptocurrencies — Investing in the Future

The cryptocurrency world is ripe with opportunities. We've discussed how Bitcoin, the most popular currency in the market, has increased its value by 5,488.11% in the last seven years (Buy Bitcoin Worldwide, 2023). Now, this technology isn't naive, and it's ripe with both risks and benefits. You stand to win a lot if you do things the right way. So let's study this asset in depth.

What Are Cryptocurrencies?

Cryptocurrency can be defined as virtual money or a virtual commodity. Either way, cryptocurrencies have certain characteristics:

1. **Virtuality:** They are fully virtual tokens, with no physical coinage.
2. **Decentralization:** They are coined by a process that's not governed by a single institution like a central bank, but by a protocol based on blockchain technology called mining. Similarly, cryptocurrency operations aren't kept in centralized journals.
3. **Deregulation:** Though there's an increasing push to regulate the technology, it's one that cannot be fully regulated.
4. **Instantaneity:** They are designed to make operations nearly instantaneously; therefore, they are ideal for cross-border operations where the legacy banking system would be too slow for payments.

5. **Immutability:** As operations are kept in decentralized ledgers, once they are recorded they cannot be reversed.

6. **Cryptographic:** Each token and operation is identified and secured through cryptography, using hash codes that include both a private and public key and a receipt of the operation. This process is called triple entry accounting, whereby operations are third-party receipts that prevent double-spending. These features allow cryptocurrencies to act as stores of value.

7. **Specific purpose:** Unlike legal tender, which is coined for trade and monetary policy purposes only, each cryptocurrency has a specific purpose. For instance, Ethereum is coined to sustain the decentralized finance industry, while Tether is coined to be a commodity pegged to the dollar.

8. **Money:** Cryptocurrencies can be used as money due to their properties and have an intrinsic value rising from the blockchain infrastructure that supports them.

There are some characteristics that aren't shared by all currencies, like having a limited amount of tokens. This is the case, for instance, with Bitcoin. Other currencies, like Ethereum, have unlimited issuance. However, no currency is issued following public policy needs but by following a protocol. Therefore, this makes cryptocurrencies deflationary by nature.

Now, let's talk about the kind of coins you might be able to find in the market. The two main cryptocurrencies on the market are Bitcoin and Ethereum. Each of these currencies has its own ledger, the Bitcoin blockchain and the Ethereum Virtual Machine. Then, there are altcoins and stablecoins, which can have their own ledger or work within the Ethereum Virtual Machine environment.

Altcoins, Ethereum, and Bitcoin work similarly in that their value is subject to market appraisal and their markets are highly volatile. Altcoins tend to be far more volatile than Bitcoin and Ethereum, so they are riskier assets and require a profound market study of each coin before investing any money in them.

Stablecoins are easier to understand. These tend to have their value pegged to a given coin or commodity in the market. These coins may be backed by fiat money, commodities, or other cryptocurrencies. The idea of having a pegged value is to offer an asset that isn't as volatile as standard cryptocurrencies. As stablecoins need to be backed, they are generally centralized by exchanges, which hold the collateral for pegged value, as is the case for Tether and USDC. That is unless the stablecoin is backed by a cryptocurrency portfolio and its value is stabilized through smart contracts, as is the case with DAI. Stablecoins are used either for payments or stabilizing a crypto portfolio when cryptocurrencies are in a bear trend.

Keep in mind that decentralization is a key aspect of cryptocurrencies. A cryptocurrency will generally be linked to a digital ledger that's open-source and has a whitepaper. The key here is competing against fiat money so that cryptocurrencies can become standardized payment methods at the level of legal tender. While some central banks push digital currencies, these should not change the equation as the monetary base of most countries is mainly digital anyway. We just hadn't had the chance to see central banks give their legal tender a flair akin to cryptocurrencies. Yet we have been seeing countries like El Salvador increasingly use cryptocurrencies as reserves for their central banks. And it's understandable: Cryptocurrencies are hardcoded, transparent social constructs. Therefore, they are quite hard to counterfeit and take down.

Risks and Benefits of Investing in Cryptocurrencies

Let's divide this into pros and cons while focusing on the investment aspect.

Pros

1. **Liquidity:** Cryptocurrency can work as either store-of-value, alternate currency, and in some cases, legal tender.

2. **Diverse volatility:** Depending on your aversion to risk, the crypto market offers a great array of volatile and stable coins that allows investors to allocate assets efficiently, and replace traditional investments. Volatility also gives the chance for portfolio appreciation.

3. **Micro-investments:** It allows small investors to get used to investing without having to contribute large amounts of money. In fact, your investment can be as small as $10. This corresponds to the fractionable nature of cryptocurrency, which can be divided as low as by the power of 10^{-8}, or eight decimal places, and even lower. Now, be mindful of buying above the gas fee or exchange fee if you aren't buying crypto fractions directly.

4. **Lower fees:** Generally, cryptocurrencies offer lower fees for mediation in transactions. Nevertheless, some shopping may be required, especially when trading on exchanges. You should keep an eye though on hidden fees or deceptive

36

practices on cheap and free fees. Nevertheless, it's quite unlikely for a cryptocurrency user to be charged beyond the publicized fees, given that the owner of the wallet is in control of the operations. If you become an expert at cryptocurrencies you could instantly transfer an amount akin to $1 billion for less than a dollar.

5. **Store of value:** Since the rules for coinage are determined by precoded events that every player is aware of, and are not subject to centralized monetary policy, cryptocurrencies tend to be deflationary assets, and helpful as a store of value in comparison to legal tender. This store of value functions as a commodity, subject to the rules of supply and demand. Furthermore, as cryptocurrency operations are secured under the triple-entry accounting protocol, these can avoid spiraling into fraud due to unchecked double-spending. Moreover, it allows building passive income under certain investment strategies like staking.

6. **24–7 accessibility**: Unlike in traditional banking and markets, the cryptocurrency market is operating 24–7 non-stop, no evening days, no holidays. You have smaller idle time than in regular financial markets. This accessibility also places cryptocurrencies as the most attractive investment in many developing countries where access to finance is impaired due to faulty financial infrastructure.

7. **Protection against fraud:** Operations with cryptocurrencies are not reversible. Therefore, they protect merchants from fraudulent chargebacks from unknown consumers. In exchange, consumers obtain irrefutable proof of their

performance, so long as they can attach the merchant's key to its personally identifiable information.

Cons

1. **Security:** Storing cryptocurrency requires a certain degree of security measures necessary to protect your wallet and private key, though this task can be delegated to a trusted exchange company.

2. **Ponzi schemes:** Especially in the alt-coin and stable-coins market, the coin issuer requires big amounts of money to maintain the system alive until the blockchain acquires a value of its own. If a given blockchain isn't backed up with sufficient money, any coin can become a Ponzi scheme, as happened with the FTX coin, and many others that preceded it.

3. **Coin freeze:** Similarly, a liquidity crisis in an exchange or a poorly established coin can cause withdrawal freezes and coin rushes. These moves can lead to bankruptcy for the companies you engage in business with, and your chances to recover your investment are reduced to that of an unsecured creditor.

4. **Loss of storage:** Cryptocurrency needs to be stored. If you lose the storage system you are using or the private key with which you access your wallet, then your investment is gone forever.

5. **Compatibility:** Cryptocurrencies work over blockchain ledgers with compatibility issues. Unless you are trading through an exchange, you may find it hard to make

transactions with third parties or liquidate your cryptocurrency holdings.

6. **Whales:** As in any other market, a concentration of cryptocurrencies with a major player can leave the market vulnerable to higher volatility. Some whale investor addresses are tracked to detect sharp moves that may destabilize any cryptocurrency's regular volatility.

7. **Pools:** There's a potential risk (albeit diminishingly low) of a 51% attack by mining pools, which may alter all the records in a given blockchain in the event of halvings or sharp drops in cryptocurrency value.

8. **Correlated volatility:** The most established cryptocurrencies, Bitcoin and Ethereum, have started to follow the S&P 500 index during the pandemic, as they lost their fringe investment status. Therefore, these currencies may not cover against a bear market unless you are following a dollar-cost-averaging strategy.

9. **Non-backed commodity:** Cryptocurrencies are commodities, and except for stablecoins, they aren't backed up by cash, dividends, or collateral. Whatever investment you hold in crypto, earnings depend on the asset's market value alone.

10. **Developing asset:** Cryptocurrencies are mostly in the beta stage, and are barely evolutions of a minimum viable product. Though useful as such, they still have a long way to go before they become a dominant technology or fulfill their potential. In fact, the technology is still pending further scaling.

11. **Quantum computing:** While this technology isn't fully developed yet, it's the only technology with the potential to

take down any blockchain supporting a cryptocurrency. However, blockchains will certainly adapt to this threat by adopting post-quantum algorithms.

Trade-offs

The cryptocurrency environment is designed to support safe, anonymous, and anarchical relationships. This should be considered a trade-off as opposed to a risk or benefit. In other words, cryptocurrency is not an environment where you'll be babysat if you plan to go beyond operating in crypto exchanges, which, as businesses, must comply with regulations. The crypto world is an environment designed to give you full risk and full control of your operations and your assets in exchange for enhanced privacy and freedom.

Cryptography and decentralization are at the heart of the cryptocurrency project in that a decentralized network has no nexus and no central server that can be attacked and annulled. If no one can collectively gather more CPU power than the whole network, then the network is fully safe and impossible to take down. And it's this decentralized peer-to-peer network that can act as a trust agent instead of a third party like a bank or a credit card company to prevent double-spending.

Another trade-off to consider is the mandatory requirement of trust agents to act as mediators between two parties. If mediation is mandatory, then your operations can be saved through reversions, but this will make every operation more costly as the risk of a reversible operation is always higher than a non-reversible operation, and the possibility of micro-operations and micro-investments is then gone.

This decentralized network has found a pretty solid way of accounting for operations: the triple-entry accounting principle. Under this principle, the operation is not only recorded as a double entry by the buyer and seller in their private journals, but also the network produces a time-stamped, cryptographically signed, and proofed receipt of the operation that is kept within the network. And thus it's the network that prevents double-spending.

Then the other key aspect is to decide how consensus is built on a decentralized network that a given operation has taken place. Here's where protocols kick in. Protocols mandate that a proof-of-work or a proof-of-stake shows that an operation has taken place when a third party cryptographically secures or validates the operation against third-party attacks. But this validating party can be anyone in the network acting as a miner, who is paid for each validated operation in bargain for the CPU resource they spend validating the operation. The trade-off is social in that decentralized mining is nowadays an energy-intensive activity, and Bitcoin's network alone accounts for an energy consumption akin to that of the Netherlands, in a market where there are more than 20,000 coins of different cryptocurrencies. Thus, investing in cryptocurrency may be potentially unsustainable in the long run due to energy and environmental constraints.

Buying, Storing, and Selling Cryptocurrencies

While private operations are a possibility, which is how Bitcoin started, most crypto transactions are handled by exchanges nowadays. You'll be purchasing through an exchange that can either be centralized or decentralized. Most beginner investors will opt for centralized exchanges due to their simplicity of use. However, one must be aware that the exchange needs to meet two requirements: being trustworthy and having enough liquidity. This is because exchanges generally function like banks with cryptocurrencies.

Let's talk a bit about fees. There are transaction costs for each operation made on a blockchain. Miners, who are in charge of maintaining a blockchain environment, earn a gas fee for recording any transaction in the blockchain. Above that, if you buy via an exchange, you are also likely to pay a commission, which is the exchange's profit for simplifying cryptocurrency management for you.

As for accessing exchanges, generally, you access a centralized exchange first, and then operate on decentralized ones. To access a centralized exchange, you'll have to comply with mandatory regulations for any financial investment, like anti-money laundering and know-your-customer policies. Then, you'll be able to send fiat money to purchase cryptocurrencies. Once you have your cryptocurrencies, you'll require a hot wallet, like MetaMask, to host your tokens online. With these wallets, you'll be able to engage with decentralized exchanges.

Crypto is stored in a wallet, which can be custodial (held by another company) or non-custodial (held by yourself). Each of these has hacking risks, but as investors advance in their technical understanding of cryptocurrencies, they generally shift towards non-custodial wallets for enhanced control and safety over cryptocurrencies owned. Now, let's see further ways of storing cryptocurrencies:

1. **Hot storage:** This is online storage, through online non-custodial or custodial wallets.
2. **Cold storage:** This is offline storage, where data is generally stored in hard drives and USB.

Then, you can also store the private key, for which there are several methods:

1. **Multisignature wallets:** You can use a multiple key system where you store your private key with different people. In this case, you'll need two or more of the total keys to validate an operation, while you hedge against the risk of loss of keys.
2. **Paper wallets:** This means keeping your keys written on paper. This method has lost its security advantages over time, so now it's a risky way of holding keys.
3. **Cloud wallets:** This is a cloud technology that can hold your wallet and keys.
4. **App wallets:** This is the methodology used by exchanges—of having online apps that can let you choose to hold custody of your key separately.
5. **Software wallets:** These are wallets and keys that can be installed in your device, yet are hot, as they are online.
6. **Hardware wallets**: These are hard drives or USBs holding your wallet cold.

There are some safety measures to implement while storing crypto, like maintaining your anonymity, using a double identification factor for validating operations, keeping your devices free of malware, diversifying wallets, using https sites only, or double-checking addresses when sending crypto to third parties outside an exchange.

The key aspect of a wallet is the mnemonic phrase or seed phrase used as a backup for the wallet. The best way of storing them is on paper, in a fireproof desk or safe, with the words numbered in order. Otherwise, the wallet may be lost forever. Any other DIY method to store a wallet is simply a bad idea, so don't do it.

While you are still a beginner at selling cryptocurrency, your go-to option will normally be an exchange. Now, if you've got the hang of selling crypto on your own, you can try decentralized exchanges or direct operations. Generally, sending crypto requires you to have two elements: your private key for sending and the receiver's address. If you have any open positions in an exchange, you may need to close them. Generally, exchanges collect fees for sending crypto and require a minimum amount. If you are investing, make sure the spread you are getting is worth a sale. If not, hold.

Now, if your idea is to sell to liquidate, you need to integrate your crypto with a payment service, like a credit card, a bank account, or digital wallets, like Paypal, Skrill, or Payoneer. Again, for liquidation, the most seamless experience is with exchanges. But not all exchanges will meet your needs, so you must analyze the integration services they offer.

Strategies for Investing in Cryptocurrencies

Let's review some basic investment strategies once again:

1. **Staking:** You can raise interest in crypto by holding and freezing your tokens for a period of time in any blockchain. This may also increase your holdings to the point where you

can utilize the Proof-of-Stake method for mining. Exchanges may offer a similar compounding service to maintain liquidity in their platforms.

  a. **Pros:** It allows gains on holding strategies.
  b. **Cons:** These coins may not be liquidated for some period of time.

2. **Cost-averaging:** This is a good investing technique for holding over time without running the risk of entering at a bad price, the key aspect is committing to buying a small price over regular intervals of time. This strategy helps to boost compounding.

  a. **Pros:** You need a smaller initial investment, can avoid entering too high, can buy at discount, are less exposed to stress, and get to understand the crypto market dynamics better.
  b. **Cons:** You miss market bottoms, take time to earn, and lose potential earnings in bull markets.

3. **Momentum:** Momentum investing is about having an entry and exit price. While out, the crypto invested in should be a stablecoin. While in, it's Bitcoin, Ethereum, or any altcoin that isn't stable. And the good news is that cryptocurrencies are far more volatile than stocks, so it's ripe for momentum trading.

  a. **Pros:** Good environment for momentum trading, with high-profit possibilities.

b. **Cons:** A market trap may cause assets to lose quickly, and gains may not surpass fees.

4. **Buy and hold:** Having in mind that Bitcoin has significantly multiplied its value over time, a buy-and-hold strategy isn't bad either, but this might be a reckless choice for altcoins. Pros and cons are similar to those of cost-averaging.

You may further automate your purchases and sales using orders like take-profit and stop-loss. These orders help you take out the emotion from decision-making, limiting your movements to those you've planned for—that is, your exit price for both winning (take-profit) and losing (stop-loss). You should never take investor profiles and emotions for granted, especially in a market as volatile as the crypto market. Automating your exit points will protect you from panic sales.

Beyond cryptocurrencies, there are crypto-related investments, including ETFs, coin trusts, and Bitcoin futures. This is an indirect sort of investment, with distributed risk but high maintenance costs in comparison with regular crypto investments. A crypto ETF will follow the stocks of the main businesses in the crypto market. A coin trust is a stake in a trust holding a cryptocurrency portfolio. A Bitcoin future is similar to a flash loan agreement, as there's an agreement for buying or selling crypto at a given price at a future date.

Arbitrage

You can also earn money by looking for price differences in cryptocurrencies, i.e. arbitrage. Understanding arbitrage in cryptocurrency markets requires understanding two elements:

volatility and exchange markets. The first reason why arbitrage is possible in a cryptocurrency environment is high volatility. High volatility impedes prices from being stable among exchanges. The second element affecting arbitrage is the existence of centralized and decentralized exchanges.

Exchanges use different pricing systems depending on whether they are centralized or decentralized. A centralized exchange uses orders to fix the price of cryptocurrencies; whereas decentralized exchanges use an automated market maker system, which uses arbitrage to make prices akin to those of centralized exchanges. But, as centralized exchanges differ in their orders, prices may differ even across them. This allows many opportunities for arbitrage:

1. Cross-exchange.
2. Cross-continent.
3. Triangulation.
4. Decentralization.

These are fairly obvious by their names, except for triangulation. In triangulation you calculate that you can increase your currency's value by a series of three conversions: A to B, B to C, and C back to A. This can be done within the same exchange.

The risks in arbitrage are significantly lower than in trading, as the investment horizon is in minutes at most, and no predictive market analysis is required to know how much you'll earn. You know as soon as you spot and calculate the discrepancy. The main hurdles you'll face are fee and timing constraints. Blockchain operations take 10 minutes to be confirmed, plus if you move large amounts of coins, you may be subject to anti-money laundering scans. Another timing risk would be an exchange going offline. The good news is that crypto arbitration can be automated.

Understanding Blockchain Technology and Its Potential Applications

If you understand that each cryptocurrency has its own specific purpose, then you may also use that purpose to boost your investments. This means that you'll be shifting from just investing in crypto to actually building a business around it. With this degree of expertise, you may build more than just your retirement portfolio; you can even build your newfound career. For that, it'll be good to start studying blockchain, the infrastructure behind cryptocurrencies.

The Blockchain

Cryptocurrencies are no more than tokens within a technology called blockchain. The blockchain is simply a decentralized ledger that uses third parties to validate operations. This validation process is called mining, as validating an operation creates a new block in the blockchain and gives the miner cryptocurrencies in exchange. Generally, a validation by six or more different miners is required for an operation to be deemed valid. As miners are paid per number of operations, they have no interest in any given operation but simply in mining as fast as possible. Also, the miners work as the guarantors of the trust system, as they all pool the ledger, so as to keep recorded transactions safe from cyberattacks.

Mining works under two types of protocols: Proof-of-Work and Proof-of-Stake. The Proof-of-Work is a more resource-intensive protocol than the Proof-of-Stake, so it's used for blockchains holding cryptocurrencies only. The prime example of this is the Bitcoin blockchain. The Proof-of-Stake protocol is used for blockchains that can support more than just currencies alone, like Ethereum.

The greatest asset of any blockchain infrastructure is the element of trust created through a combination of privacy and transparency. Your identity in the blockchain isn't your personal data, but your wallet's address. So long as your address isn't successfully tied to your name or you aren't required to comply with Know-Your-Customer policies, you'll remain pretty unknown. However it's this very address that is kept recorded in a transaction or blockchain node in a public, safe, and decentralized manner.

Blockchains may also be layered to simplify mining. While the blockchain is a highly efficient way of facilitating cross-border transactions, this technology can easily be overloaded with multiple transactions occurring at the same time. Layering is the use of different blockchains to preprocess operations so that the native or Layer 1 blockchain isn't overloaded.

Given the mining protocol and blockchain design, a blockchain may hold more than just tokens as assets. Such is the case of the Ethereum Virtual Machine, which is the blockchain behind Ethereum. This blockchain is a state machine rather than a ledger, and as such, it can store both tokens and smart contracts while integrating with other blockchains.

Smart contracts may be the greatest innovation in blockchain technology. These are basically agreements that are executed in code once a condition is met. The idea behind smart contracts is to protect contract privity and credit. Under privity, contracts are meant to be a relationship that affects the involved parties only. But for that to happen, credit, that which is owed and the collateral used to secure it, needs to be automated so that you needn't resort to a third party to enforce credit, like a court, a guarantor, or a trustee. Again, the key here is using the blockchain for triple-entry accounting. Still, the market around these contracts needs to be developed further.

This technology may automate workflows, and help build trust in key areas, like pharmaceutics, retailers, international trade, food supply, and finance. Moreover, smart contracts support the technology behind decentralized financing and decentralized applications, which encompass the ambitious Web3 project.

The Web3 Project

Web3 is an internet decentralization project through blockchain technology. The underlying idea is a return to privacy and stakeholding that's been lost with all the current centralized internet infrastructure. It's simply the origins of Bitcoin—that is, recovering privacy in transactions, but on steroids. Yet the project is still in its infancy, and the real potential of using blockchain infrastructure to support the web is unknown. This means there are a lot of opportunities for growth and investment. The key here is using a crypto wallet as the single identity data of any stakeholder.

For any app to meet web3 standards, the design must allow for technical, economic, and legal decentralization. Technical decentralization is achieved by using blockchain technology to support operations. Now, not any blockchain is capable of supporting a decentralized economy. Only blockchains that are programmable, like Ethereum, Avalanche, and Solana, may support communities with a decentralized economy. The key here is using code to invest users with power so that they can add value to the decentralized economic environment.

The legal decentralization aspect, though, is a bit harder to achieve. To start with, a web3 system would need to have no asymmetric information, which is a scenario where there's a party with privileged information, as it happens with centralized entities in web2. While the open-source nature of web3 impedes asymmetry by having all information regarding a project be public and copy-left (this is, with authorization to read, copy and write), that doesn't mean that users are fully aware of or understand the platform. Then there are proprietary rights that can't be held in a decentralized fashion. Hence, many web3 apps have not-for-profit corporations that hold assets that can't be decentralized.

Now the reality is that open-source technologies have been on the market for a while, mainly server-side and in smartphones. And it's possible that blockchain, or distributed ledger, open-source projects may be in the background of much of our hardware and apps. What open-source brings is transparency, which is ideal for a trustless system. If everyone knows how a web3 project works, then anyone who's interested in a project can enter as a user or a collaborator.

Web3 projects are characterized as having five layered protocols:

1. **Layer 0:** This foundational layer includes cross-chain and parachain technologies, like Polkadot. Parachain technologies allow users to contribute directly to a blockchain's infrastructure by implementing a relay blockchain that can be used to communicate among different parallel blockchains and avoid bottlenecks through parallel processing. Cross-chains enable communication and operation between different, unrelated blockchains. This layer also includes peer-

to-peer internet protocols, and platform-neutral languages that enable interoperability between different operating systems.

2. **Layer 1:** This layer would include actual blockchains, which will support decentralization. As decentralization per se occurs here, then data distribution protocols will be implemented taking special account of transient and permanent data. Known data distribution and messaging protocols include IPFS, BigcharmDB, Swarm, Matrix, and Whisper.

3. **Layer 2:** This layer enables encryption, scalability, and distributed computing. Through encryption, both security and privacy functions are enabled. Scalability is also ensured by having networks that differentiate transient from permanent data, and write only the latter in the blockchain. Examples of this are Bitcoin's Lightning Network and Ethereum's Lightning Network.

4. **Layer 3:** This includes APIs and programming languages for interacting with the lower layers. The most known languages are Solidity and Vyper, which are used for Ethereum's blockchain. DApps, wallets, and even games reside on this layer.

5. **Layer 4:** This would include UIs for the blockchain, accessible from a browser. An example is the hot wallet MetaMask.

That's the basic technology stack with which web3 applications would be developed. But for now, a baby web3 will start by copying some web2 applications at a small scale. For instance, social media platform Minds is the web3 counterpart to Facebook. This social media sells itself as a platform that will not profit from the divide, as they are not interested in isolating social speech. This social media has its own token Minds, an ERC-20 token, built according to Ethereum's standard protocols for tokens. The idea of this web3 app is to allow both off-chain and on-chain transactions, where users choose how to offset security, speed, and fees. The value proposed by the Minds platform is to prevent algorithm manipulation that shadowbans content creators, and manage centralization and secrecy, which lead to surveillance and censorship policies, including deplatforming and demonetization.

As token rewards are hardcoded into a smart contract, demonetization or deplatforming are impossible. And algorithm manipulation will be impossible, as now advertising will be managed with peer-to-peer services like Boost (decentralized ads) and Wire (decentralized payments), meaning that the users will be dealing with advertising parties directly. The only centralized aspect of the platform is that it's being hosted within Amazon's AWS.

The Web3 Environment

For a project like Web3 to work, decentralized property rights had to be created. Those are known as non-fungible tokens (NFTs). An NFT is simply an encrypted certificate of property over a digital asset, which is kept on the blockchain as a public record. With property rights come stakeholding and community building, which are the main interests of Web3 developers. NFTs can also be used for investments; , one investment in the artist known as Beeple rose to $6.6 million (Kastrenakes, 2021), meaning art may have a promising future with NFTs.

NFTs became popular with the rise of profile pics (PFPs) and avatar collections for social media profile pictures. Of these, the Bored Ape Yacht Club collection is the one that made the news not so long ago. The idea of PFPs is to prove that your profile picture is a piece of original artwork. Consider it like owning the Mona Lisa and having it on your dining room wall rather than in the Louvre. And the best part is that it's possible to prove the authenticity of ownership due to the blockchain. Social media platforms have made alliances with NFT platforms, like Twitter and Open Sea, to track NFT authenticity and provide a special badge to those who publish a PFP as a profile picture in their social media.

The process of minting artwork into an NFT and releasing it is called a drop. This is a primary sale, in that the artists register the artwork into the Ethereum Virtual Machine by paying ETH upfront (minting) or deferring ETH payment to the first purchase (lazy minting). Then, the NFT goes for sale on the secondary market, where it's sold and resold. Artists with an audience may use platforms to program drops with two big features: allowlists and releases. Allowlists permit pre-purchase of NFTs before the public sale date, whereas releases show the NFTs with generic artwork, where the generic placeholder hypes the unique piece. The NFT is then updated with a unique piece of artwork. A release is ideal for card collections and similar products that are dropped as a series.

Through smart contracts and NFTs, it's possible to build applications. Such is the case with decentralized applications (dApps) and decentralized gaming. For instance, in a game like Axie Infinity, it's possible to play and invest, and a given parcel of land was once sold for $1.1 million (Chow, 2021). By having ownership rights and stakeholding, apps can be turned upside down. For instance, in gaming, there's downloadable content. But that content isn't something you truly own or can create value with, it's just a service owned by the developer. With NFTs, you get to be a stakeholder in downloadable content, so now a player may own a game's assets. Now, dApps can also power financing platforms, lotteries, and streaming services, among other uses. However, there's still a long way to go with dApps, especially in matters of security, as an open-source network is easier to hack while it's still in development. But with time, these platforms can become rock solid in terms of security and performance once they are established.

With dApps, you can also support decentralized autonomous organizations (DAOs). You may think of DAOs as decentralized corporations run by stakeholders rather than by a board of directors. These use smart contracts for implementing their decision making so that no decision may be overturned. These organizations are built on blockchain technology and spread through spontaneous pitches to raise funds for diverse purposes, both within and outside the cryptocurrency market. The key phase in any DAO is the design of the smart contract infrastructure, so that no vulnerabilities may jeopardize the project. Once a project is launched, developers become just another stakeholder among many. The key here is using the blockchain for transparent decision-making, thus removing the need for trust among stakeholders.

These DAOs have limited wriggle room and, therefore, aren't suitable for commercial activity, which is about making decisions through planning and on the fly. DAOs only allow planned and agreed-on decisions to be implemented. So far there's little regulation on DAOs. In the State of Wyoming, these have been regulated and granted a status akin to LLCs, whereas if not regulated, they'd be treated as a general partnership with unlimited liability.

An interesting example of a DAO is CityDAO, which works around the notion of decentralized citizenship and ownership of land. To be a citizen, a person must join the CityDAO guild or purchase a token in the secondary market. Then, citizens may propose and vote on citizen projects and raise funds to implement them. So far, this project has managed to legally purchase two parcels of land—one in Wyoming, and one in Colorado—whose property rights have been tokenized as an NFT. The key idea here is to choose citizenship rather than get one for being born there. Or as the CityDAO's citizens believe: It's easier to build a new city from scratch than reform an already established one.

The final leg of the web3 movement is decentralized finance (DeFi), which started with the Bitcoin boom. DeFi is about privacy, accessibility, and finances. Central banks are a big problem nowadays, especially with lackluster monetary policy leading to inflation. Not even the US seems to be able to bring down inflation in the post-Covid era. DeFi has given inflation-laden countries access to savings via stablecoins.

Other services that made DeFi more attractive are faster cross-border transactions and streamlined payments via smart contracts. All this technology has made contracts more secure worldwide. Moreover, accessing credit has become easier, as most loans are now given at real-time interest rates with only collateral as a qualification requirement. Also, you may lend money on interest through staking dApps. And loans like flash loans can be investment opportunities to earn money on the spread of selling cryptocurrency, akin to an option contract. Further services include index funds for your cryptocurrency portfolio, portfolio management, insurance, and crowdfunding, among others.

A DAO/DeFi project that is widely popular is MakerDAO. This project is behind the stablecoin DAI. The governance token is the MKR, with which you are entitled to participate in the decision-making process around the Maker Protocol and DAI's risks. Therefore MakerDAO is what stabilizes DAI's price. The Maker Protocol is a dApp developed in the Ethereum Virtual Machine that allows the creation and stabilization of DAIs. However, not all aspects of MakerDAO are fully decentralized; hence, it's supported by two corporations. The Maker Foundation is responsible for launching the Maker Protocol together with associated third parties and for carrying out the decentralization of MakerDAO to the fullest extent possible. The DAI Foundation is responsible for housing MakerDAO's intangibles, such as IP rights, and other assets that cannot be decentralized.

As of now, MakerDAO has implemented multiple collateralizations of DAI, through coins existing in the Ethereum environment, as agreed upon by MKR holders. The key value of DAI is that blockchain technology allows for a transparent reduction of DAI's volatility in comparison to central bank policy. DAI has also spurred the creation of public and private centralized currencies by organizations that may hold institutional trust—like JP Morgan or the Central Bank of China—yet lack MakerDAO's transparency.

The underlying technology consists of automated market makers, which are dApps that ensure there's enough liquidity among currencies to make the trade without price slippages. Smart contracts are employed to create liquidity pools of the assets to be exchanged and replace middlemen in the exchange operation. Only, anyone in the DeFi network can be a liquidity provider instead of a centralized entity. So the big risk in these exchanges is that a pool lacks sufficient liquidity. The other risk, especially for liquidity providers, is a change in pool ratio. If the provider doesn't stop losses, he'll have a permanent loss. Otherwise, the loss is impermanent, as the ratio may be recovered. Participating in decentralized exchanges as a pooler or trader provides tokens that grant DAO votes and can be staked to earn interest. A well-known decentralized exchange is Uniswap, an Ethereum-based DAO using UNI tokens.

With all these possibilities within reach of any blockchain environment, a good way to know whether your investment will work or not is to carefully read through whitepapers and understand the project behind each specific blockchain or cryptocurrency you intend to invest in. If the project is too far away from achievement or poorly planned, then it's best to steer clear of that cryptocurrency in particular.

The Competition to Blockchain

While most cryptocurrencies build their distributed ledger technologies on the blockchain, others have decided to use direct acyclical graphs (DAGs) as their underlying technologies. Instead of using a chain of blocks, each transaction can individually validate other transactions without using mining protocols, which thus allows for operations below the fee threshold with the goal of supporting a higher frequency of transactions. DAGs also look for scalability by allowing multiple parent blocks and parallel validation of operations while impeding blocks from referring to their immediate predecessor block, so that no operation is registered on a cycle or overwritten. These two features should make DAGs a less resource intensive technology. These currencies, however, still depend on a coordinator role for validating transactions, as DAGs are more vulnerable to alterations than blockchains, meaning that their decentralization is yet to be achieved, as is the case with IOTA and Hedera.

A further limitation of blockchain technology is that, as it works with single parent nodes, it can't host all operations and needs to discard those that haven't reached sufficient consensus. In fact, mining protocols are designed to cause bottlenecks that slow down operations in order to guarantee their security. Yet consensus in blockchains isn't final, but probable. In DAG structures, it's possible to reach final consensus through an asynchronous Byzantine Fault Tolerant system, where a ⅔ majority of votes validates the operation. However, this system, though final, may not be as secure as blockchain protocols.

Blockchain and DAG hint at a trilemma: ensuring scalability, decentralization, and security. While blockchain is decentralized and secure, it remains hard to scale, as most operations need to refer to a single parent node, and the consensus mechanism is energy intensive. Conversely, DAG is easier to scale but hard to decentralize and secure. Layer 2s are the answer for scalability to blockchain bottlenecks, and sacrifice scalability in favor of the other two. Meanwhile, DAGs are still developing their decentralization and security features and still require a coordinator to revalidate operations.

Navigating the Cryptocurrency Regulatory Landscape

Cryptocurrency has been in the eye of regulators for a long time, especially as the DeFi market ethos implies competition against centralization, and the cryptocurrency market has an inherent risk of harming consumers and financing illegal activity. And the problem is that the worldwide approach isn't in unison. Some regulate legal uses of crypto; others forbid using crypto as a purchase method. Meanwhile, the only advanced legislation worldwide regarding cryptocurrencies is anti money laundering.

As of now, the biggest piece of legislation in effect is the EU's MiCA (Markets in Crypto Assets), which aims to stabilize volatility in the crypto market. It regulates aspects like e-money issuance, stablecoin reserves, and credit lending by e-money institutions and crypto asset services, where e-money can stand as a central digital currency, like a digital euro. The policymakers in the EU have seen that volatility is high, especially among Proof-of-Stake coins and stablecoins, which generally have liquidity crises as a consequence of unregulated lending practices, coin runs, and market volatility. The least risky assets, in their view, include NFTs, DeFi, and Proof-of-Work coins.

The main agencies in the US that monitor cryptocurrencies are the Financial Crimes Enforcement Network, the Securities Exchange Commission, and the Commodity Futures Trading Commission. Under US regulations, cryptocurrency is regarded as an instrument for payment (as a substitute for money), security (collateral), and commoditization. Exchanges are subject to anti money laundering policies, anti fraud scans, and stablecoin reserve policies. However, as of 2022, there isn't an encompassing national legislation, but a corpus of disjointed state laws (PwC, 2022). There's a project for digital US dollars issued by the Federal Reserve, but it's still undergoing feasibility research. However, coin offerings are required to be publicized in compliance with the requirements of the Securities Exchange Commission.

The most famous policy regarding the crypto market is anti money laundering (AML). Through this policy, cryptocurrency exchanges control their customer base to track any activity suspicious of criminal intent or money laundering. It is based on keeping customer data based on risk-profile protocols, restricting access to politically exposed people, and checking that customers aren't facing international sanctions. The key number to watch out for is transactions above $10,000. Also, exchanges that engage in mixing or tumbling for the purpose of obscuring the transparency of operations within the crypto market have been fined by the Financial Crimes Enforcement Network by amounts of up to $60 million for not complying with AML regulations (Lemire, 2022).

However, despite AML policy, it'd be hard to affirm that it's easy to finance illegal activities through cryptocurrency. For starters, paper cash is still the most private way of making transactions. Secondly, most criminal activities are financed via cash or wire transfers. Finally, cryptocurrencies are impossible to forfeit, which reduces by half the amount of criminal activity that could be done through them.

As a push to decrease risk in cryptocurrency transactions, exchange platforms have started to implement know-your-customer policies, by which personally identifiable information is gathered from each customer. While this contradicts the privacy-first model of cryptocurrencies, it also serves as a prevention against criminal activity. Likewise, businesses are required to implement know-your-business policies, by which agencies worldwide keep records on the stakeholders behind all crypto exchanges.

While policy may help prevent increasing scams around the crypto market, it's ideal to keep in mind that investments will be closely monitored. Therefore, getting counsel from an accountant on how to handle tax-related issues with cryptocurrencies might be a good starting point to protect your portfolio. For instance, in the US, cryptocurrency transactions are treated as property transactions for taxation purposes, and the value of the currency at the date of trade must be included in tax returns. No exemptions such as foreign currency operations may be applied. However, there's still a lack of criteria by the IRS to properly value taxable gains or losses. As for state taxes, the criteria aren't unified. Hence, the need for counsel.

As you can see, all the regulations are in contradiction with the cryptocurrency ethos, which is a privacy-first environment. If your wallet address is linked to your personally identifiable information, then your privacy is gone forever. What most privacy advocates do is hold two different wallets: one for personal operations that is unidentifiable, and the other for exchange purposes, used primarily to convert cryptocurrency into legal tender.

Furthermore, the regulation doesn't necessarily meet the needs of decentralization in that it catches up slowly with technology and is always imperfect. Also, regulation is centralized and devised to have a close relationship with centralized private industry, where there's feedback between regulators and companies. Basically, as regulation is always playing a catch-up game, the regulations work for building trustworthiness rather than building from truth.

And that's the weak spot in centralization: you trust, but you never know. Basically, only the central entity is in control. Regulatory bodies and users may only use, hope, and react. Now, open-source means permissionless. If you see that you need permission, then that's a red flag for investing in web3 technologies. Blockchain just brings a rule-based opportunity for great economic achievements. And it can do that because it's a social construct based on code. As you might have heard, *code is law*. Only that, with blockchain, this law doesn't build trust but truth. But for truth to be spread, it has to be open and permissionless. If no one can know what a blockchain will do, then perhaps the asset is best kept centralized and on Web2, and in the worst of cases, it's flagging a scam, which unfortunately has happened around fake altcoins and fake exchanges.

Chapter 4: Putting It All Together—Creating a Personalized Investment Plan

Now that you get the gist of the cryptocurrency market, let's integrate cryptocurrencies into our investing endeavors, starting with designing our own investment plan.

Personalizing the Investment Plan

An investment plan starts with two key data:

1. Your current situation
2. Your investment goals

With these two elements, you can start building and personalizing an investment plan. Without them, you are prone to acquiring assets with the hope of getting a quick, one-off profit—a neuroscience gap that most scammers love to exploit—which fills the occasional investor with false hope. Your true goal, retiring early, will be the sole focus of your investment plan.

Then, from your current situation, you would define:

1. Your expected cash reserves
2. Your emergency fund

This means that your investments will not necessarily start with cryptocurrencies. And if they do, it should be through stablecoins, Bitcoin, or Ethereum in a dollar cost averaging strategy. After that, you will assess your investment profile. Remember this table for simple guidance, but fine-tune it according to your allocation strategy.

Let's look at some crypto-related assets, classified by risk and strategy investment, where buy-and-hold and DCA include a staking or compounding strategy if possible.

Remember that the wealth-building phase should be at the beginning towards the mid-stage of your investment cycle, so you should start as aggressively as your investor profile allows. However, to build wealth you need cash for cushioning those investments. Hence, why I insist on cash reserves. Once you are closer to the retirement goal, in time and money, your strategy should downscale into conservative mode, so you protect the earnings you fought hard for and have them as liquid as possible for those free days of your life.

Now, the other leg of your investment plan is properly allocating cryptocurrency. Let's consider for a while only your crypto portfolio, as the common tip is to invest no more than 5–10% in this kind of asset, but if you are savvy with this market, you could invest a greater portfolio allocation than that.

The best cryptocurrency diversification strategy is to invest in coins that have different use cases. Remember when we discussed that each cryptocurrency is coined with a specific purpose? If each coin in your portfolio has a different use, then it follows that their volatility won't be in sync. Multiplicity of use also entails multiplicity of industries. So, you have a pretty solid starting point here. Make sure that the cryptocurrency's use case is somewhat aligned with your investment strategy. If you aren't willing to do the research, then search for coin trusts or just copy trade any solid investment strategy.

The next diversification strategy is the most widely used, and it involves investing in both a volatile and a stable coin. This is the cryptocurrency version of investing in stocks and bonds. With this diversification strategy, you can perform a solid rebalancing every time your portfolio is out of balance.

Another diversification strategy is investing by market cap. There are three tiers. On the big cap, you have both Bitcoin and Ethereum, as well as any coin above the $10 billion cap. On the middle cap, you have coins above the $1 billion cap, and anything below it is small cap. The lower the cap, the more risky (but not necessarily volatile) the investment.

Tracking Progress Toward Investment Goals

According to your plan, you'll be tracking certain elements:

1. Your yearly goal
2. Your ultimate goal
3. Your allocation goal

Consider a seven-year market cycle when investing. During this cycle, a risky asset is set to outperform a low-risk one, while in the short term, the low-risk asset outperforms the risky one. If your ultimate savings goal falls within the next seven years, then you should be shifting from risky to low-risk assets. This means that your allocation goal can be aggressive at first and conservative at the end. However, for this allocation strategy to succeed, you'll need the guts to stomach risky investments at the start of your road to financial freedom.

There are three main ways to track your investments:

1. **Robo advisors:** The purpose behind using advisors is to gain perspective. A hot stock may be both attractive and damaging for your goals; a slow compounding strategy might be unattractive but the right way to go. And with a robo advisor, you can add automation to your investments.
2. **Spreadsheets:** With spreadsheets, you will take a DIY approach to investing. While you may make some mistakes along the way, you'll have agency in fulfilling your goals.
3. **Apps:** Investments are generally tracked through budgeting apps. This corresponds to the fact that any investment plan starts with your current situation and to the money you are willing to invest for your retirement.

If your go-to strategy is trading, you should try journaling. Note all the specifics of your trade, like the asset, date, expected outcome, real outcome, and reasoning behind your forecast. This will help you learn from your mistakes.

Rebalancing a Portfolio

Rebalancing is simply stabilizing a portfolio to minimize risks. This is something that ought to be done every now and then to ensure that asset allocation is stabilized. Generally, portfolios are out of balance due to performance issues. For instance, a small investment in crypto for a buy and hold strategy may get out of phase with your stablecoin strategy given the proportion you allocated to each, forcing you to sell crypto to buy more stablecoins.

Now, rebalancing is something to do periodically, given your predefined strategy, and not in response to market crises. Never panic, but invest with a cool head. And this periodic rebalancing should take place once an imbalance threshold is surpassed (don't fix what ain't broken), you have the cash to support fees and costs of changing assets, and you've figured out taxation.

Considering market cycles is important to understanding investments, particularly those in relation to stocks, like crypto-ETFs. Knowing the phases of the stock market, especially of the S&P 500 index, matters to any cryptocurrency investment strategy, given that Bitcoin is starting to get in sync with the stock market, and altcoins tend to react to Bitcoin's volatility.

And the key factor behind these cycles: interest rate hikes and cuts. These may mark the start of a bear or bull cycle. While we monitor this trend, we'll know when it's best to hold and when to sell. At least when we go with a buy-and-hold strategy. For trading, it's important for reassessing entry and exit points.

The last cycle ended in 2020, with the pandemics, which paved the path for a bearish market, with a bubble created around the companies that had the most impact during the forced digitization that occurred as a result of social distancing policies and a double-digit inflation scenario in the US, to which the Fed reacted with interest rate hikes. In this scenario, a bear market may cause you to decide to buy and hold if you are young and can wait for the trend to revert to a bull market or to swap to debt instruments and stablecoin staking if you are getting closer to your retirement date.

As for Bitcoin, market cycles are a bit shorter, somewhere around two to four years. The last Bitcoin cycle started in 2018, and it's still ongoing. It's a maturity cycle, as Bitcoin became a mainstream investment after becoming a legitimate institutional investment the last time. The market peaked at $64,000, faced a correction, and now it's gradually increasing from the $18,000 bottom. But there might still not be signs of a bearish cycle or of an accumulation phase preceding the next halving event estimated between February and June 2024.

While Bitcoin may be somewhat in sync with the S&P 500, its cycles depend more on halving events (issuance events) than on interest rate hikes or cuts by a central bank. A halving event makes the ten-minute regular creation of Bitcoin blocks decrease by half. We are at a current rate of 6.25 BTC block creation, and it'll half to 3.125 BTC, when the next bull period is set to occur. This means that by the end of 2023, it'll be a good opportunity for buying-and-holding, to sell somewhere in 2024–2025.

Managing Investment Risks

Let's take a look at how to manage risks in your investments. Try to implement these as you grow closer to your retirement goal so as to protect the value you've raised.

1. **Short v. long term:** In the short term, you'll want strict rules on when to buy and sell. It doesn't matter if you are going for momentum or dollar cost averaging, you'll need investment rules so that emotion doesn't get in the way. In the long term, the strategy is just to hold until you retire. And since we are at that game, you are likely to hold.

2. **Backup money:** If you are into momentum investing, you need backup money, especially to cover for bad entries or exits. If you go all in with momentum trading and lose, you won't have a cushion to mitigate the effects of losses. There's a moment for investing and a moment for increasing cash

reserves. Be wise about having your cash reserves set before investing.

3. **Stabilizing exits:** This might be especially necessary when investing in crypto, as a countermeasure against volatility. We've discussed before how in trading, it's key to stake stablecoins in the interlude between the exit curve and the entry curve to prevent loss of value and compound on cryptocurrencies.

4. **True diversification:** When investing in coin trust, ETFs, altcoins, stablecoins, and other kinds of similar investments, it's best to check that our diversification is done through assets that are clearly different from each other. For instance, two ETFs on crypto stocks may not be that diversified, while an ETF on the S&P 500 and another in the crypto market are truly diversified. The same goes for coin trusts—check there's true diversification in their composition.

5. **Decreasing volatility:** Since our strategy includes cryptocurrency, a highly volatile asset, it's good to have low-risk assets to balance them. Using stablecoins as a counterpoint to Bitcoin, Ethereum, and altcoins is a good strategy. Keep in mind to rebalance every time the allocation is off.

6. **Consistent investments:** Use dollar-cost averaging to offset the risk of trading or simply buying and holding.

7. **Assessing your profile:** Check your investor profile constantly, and modify it according to your asset allocation strategy.

8. **Set your max loss:** This is a simple calculation: The less you lose, the less you need to recover. Don't invest in losing assets if they are in free fall. In fact, let go of them. In Bitcoin investing, that risk can be 2% below the entry price, and the exit can be automated with a stop-loss.

9. **Set your max gain:** The idea is getting rid of the fear of missing out, even when we actually resign true profits. There's a level beyond which it's not safe to keep if one is in trading. In Bitcoin investing, that can be 6% above the entry price, and the exit can be automated with a take-profit.

The idea behind these measures is to prevent any loss of assets at the wrong time and at the wrong rate, which could lead your investment efforts astray. These are the risks you'll generally need to mitigate against:

1. **Interest rates:** A rise in rates lowers your portfolio value and increases liquidity, while a cut generates the opposite effect.

2. **Market:** As we've discussed, there are market cycles. It's hard to expect winning value in a bear market, in which case, you'll be better off with less volatile assets, but a market in an accumulation phase before a bull market will be the proper time for buying and holding, so as to trade once the market is back to bull.

3. **Inflation:** Of course, with rising interest rates not only do you have a bear market on the way, but also inflation. In such a case, you must aim for returns higher than the inflation rate. Else, you'll be playing a lose-less game.

4. **Credit:** Most investments, especially those that are cataloged as low risk, are just credit. And you need the lender to have the liquidity to pay up capital plus interest, or else your debt portfolio will plummet to zero. Diversifying low-risk instruments matter, especially if you are working with stablecoins, which generally depend on an exchange's liquidity.

5. **Investment horizon:** Then, there's the risk that you may no longer work, and you'll be forced to retire sooner than expected. Against this, there's no defense better than starting as aggressively as possible, so that the shift to a conservative investment covers your retirement wage as close as the goal you've planned for.

Common Investing Mistakes

Let's look at some common investing mistakes and how to avoid them:

1. **Past alone:** You must also look to the future, the trends, and the expected returns. This is key if you are expecting to win the momentum game. Otherwise, you'll find yourself buying high and selling low. To counter this, you should have a dollar cost average and a momentum strategy applied in tandem, so that risks are balanced.

2. **Investing above possibilities:** Your cash reserves are limited, and investments tend to have risk behind it, especially if you go for momentum investing with volatile assets.

3. **Ignoring insurance:** Whatever investment you make, try to have it insured either company- or client-side. If not, hold the

investment at home and away from the intermediary, such as in a cold wallet in the case of cryptocurrency.

4. **Bad allocation:** You could say that investing in crypto more than you can back is quite silly, but even sillier is not to have crypto at all. So, by now you should have allocation rules for your crypto portfolio.

5. **Skipping the whitepaper:** Each cryptocurrency has a whitepaper explaining how the currency works and its potential to provide value to the web3 or decentralization market. A poorly written whitepaper may signal a potential scam, and reading will help you decide the best crypto for you. This is akin to not reading the initial offering of any stock or trust, and completely ignoring the benefits. The only reason you could skip the whitepaper is that you are investing in a legacy cryptocurrency.

6. **Ignoring the community:** In the crypto market there are two kinds of communities: those who believe in the web3 project, in the Cypherpunk ethos, and those who believe in getting rich quick. Cryptocurrency is a high-complexity, high-value market, with a solid vision. If this vision is missing around that coin, and it's all about winning money fast, you'll be investing in a Ponzi scheme. Also, cryptocurrencies are open source and have git repositories. If their git isn't available online or is rarely updated, then don't invest there.

7. **Investing on guaranteed income:** The only investment with guaranteed income is a certificate of deposit. All other investments have risks. If any investment outside of a certificate of deposit guarantees you an income, run away

from it. Equally wise, if you are paid for referrals only, run away from there, that's a pyramidal scheme.

8. **Feeling over planning**: It's tempting to try and beat the market, or be up-to-date and moving along with the market sentiment, but the reality is that the market moves chaotically. If you go along with market sentiment on a daily basis instead of following a well-thought plan, then brace yourself for a big crash.

9. **Being trendy:** Every now and then a one-off chance arises, like the GameStop stock crisis in 2022. But by the time you get into the hype, the train is gone. Just stick to solid investment planning and resist acting upon the fear of missing out.

10. **Following tips:** The idea of investing in a given asset out of the blue, just because it was recommended by an expert, especially on social media, is just a bad idea. Remember, if you want to try an asset out, you need to study it and see how it fits your investment strategy.

11. **Being impatient:** It takes time for a portfolio to grow and, most times, it'll go up and down like a syzygy without a clear direction, until time and solid investment let your assets grow adequately.

12. **Unclear goals:** A roadmap needs a destiny, and your destiny just can't be more money. It's a fuzzy goal, and it won't give you the kick you need to retire. You need a clear goal for both accountability and commitment.

13. **Keeping up with the Joneses:** Fear of missing out is prevalent among people who don't want to feel out of a social

sphere of advantageous people. But remember, retiring early is about what you truly want. If you invest to show off social status without this status being a key part of your plan, you might as well end up eating up your worth of unfulfilling vanity and fall prey to lifestyle creeps.

14. **High-tech frenzy:** That a new tech is in vogue doesn't mean it's a sustainable investment. That's why we've also hinted at reading whitepapers. This is because you'll be entering into a highly volatile investment, and you need to account for it in your portfolio. If such an investment is pushed by peer pressure rather than your plan, you'll be keeping up with the Joneses rather than investing for your retirement. It's this frenzy that causes bubbles, so be watchful.

15. **Not investing:** By now you know that every time you choose not to invest, you are losing purchasing power to inflation. How do you plan to retire early if you stand idle? Big or small, just start now!

Now we know what to look out for. But what does it really mean to be a disciplined investor?

1. **Playing by the book:** Set up your plan, make it realistic, and stick by it. Be sure to regularly review your plan so you aren't led astray. In fact, investors who play by the book tend to feel more confident overall, have their emergency fund, carry no debt, consider their risk tolerance when investing, and feel financially stable.

2. **Investing now:** The key to finances is compounding. Even when you don't earn interest you may compound through

dollar cost averaging and the compound annual growth rate. But for compounding to work it needs time. The sooner you invest, the better results you'll obtain. And if you are trading, you need to be consistent as well. Every day you are out because you predict a market high or low, you are losing the chance to increase your value.

3. **Playing for the long term:** Differentiate investments that will give returns in the long run, and that aren't trendy but classic. These are the ones that will meet your investment goals when the time comes. All other things are just noise and will make nothing but play with your fear of missing out and jeopardizing your winning game.

4. **Avoiding the graveyard:** Go for funds that aren't chasing the trend or trying to beat the market, just look for reasonable investments. Most funds tend to die out due to bad management or being over-ambitious. Stick with those that aim for longevity.

5. **Bringing something new:** Any time you add a strategy or an asset to your portfolio it must give you something you don't have. Otherwise, you'll just have more of the same. This is key for diversification, which is the go-to strategy in that it's impossible to predict which will be the greatest asset of the year. The past is gone and it reflects little of the present and the future. The market is that volatile.

6. **Aiming for the big three:** Any time you focus on an asset or strategy in your portfolio it must either (a) increase returns, (b) reduce volatility, or (c) get you closer to your retirement goal. The truth is that while stocks and volatile crypto will

increase your returns in the long run, this case isn't true for recessions. It takes time for these assets to recover from drops. Make your recovery faster by using assets akin to cash and bonds.

7. **Shopping for taxes and fees:** The reality is that it's already too hard to curb inflation, and building an investment strategy that increases your value takes effort and time. Don't let fees and taxes stand in your way. If your investment horizon is beyond 20 years, you'll be better off with tax-deferred investments.

8. **Rebalancing regularly:** Your planned asset allocation is there for you to prevent risks. If you don't let go of those unbalanced assets, you'll be more exposed to market shocks and crises.

So now, you have a solid plan and adequate tools to retire early. Shall we go on?

Conclusion: Investing in Your Future

Youth is potential. The things you do now may seem small, but they'll compound big in the future. And in a way, retirement is the mother of all financial milestones. Now is the time to be daring. You can't risk it at 60 as you can do in your 20s. There's just no room for that. And this isn't because old is bad, but inflation is ugly, and compounding is a good thing that only works with time.

The power of good financial habits is what will get you closer to your desired retirement goal. Habits like reviewing your finances, setting meaningful goals, sticking to a budget, increasing income streams, setting up an emergency fund, paying off debt, and being open about money, will give you great relief and confidence, with which you'll build a great future for yourself.

Now, you might be in a later stage of your life—you can save and invest, yes. And you may even achieve great financial feats. But the potential for this is lower. Time just makes things easier if you are eager to start and patient enough to wait for the results. The magic that'll get you there is compounding, letting your investments pay themselves off. So, don't let time pass away for a life of regret or astronomic grinding to get to retirement. Investing earlier is just the easy path.

A young investor is more daring tech-wise. Most older investors still work on sentiment. Younger generations understand how technology can bring untainted eyes to their investment strategy, and avoid making mistakes out of fear of missing out. Fear is an emotion that can cause crippling paralysis or heightened excitement that can make you lose money for not daring to invest or for getting behind a one-off investment that's likely to cause you to lose money.

Generally, journaling, or watching your every step in investment, is how you get your emotions in check. You may feel like belonging when chasing the hot trade, but your real belonging is among the ranks of the early retired. Don't miss out on the chance to retire out of fear.

From crypto to robo advisors, the investing world has never seen more accessibility than today. Crypto allows you to invest as little as $5 to $10 so that you might test the waters. Long gone are the days of needing to store big amounts of cash, taking a long time to get a feel for investing, or conducting extended market studies. Technology has made investing easier than ever. You only need to get your act together and put that idle penny to work for your retirement.

And it's not just money but engagement and impact. The rise of web3 is a good opportunity for you to be an early adopter of an economic sector that's bound to grow exponentially. You might have missed the big chance of leveraging an early entry into Bitcoin, but you are still in time to enter the decentralized world. And the best of it is that it plays to your abilities. Are you an artist? Consider NFTs. Are you a social actor? Consider DAOs. Are you a big trader? Consider DEXs. Consider how great your journey to early retirement can be.

Don't wait until it's too late; you can start now!

Appendix: Resources for Further Learning

Here's a list of recommended books, websites, and other resources for young adults interested in investing, retiring early, and navigating cryptocurrencies.

Books

1. ***On Investing Well: The Elements of Good Investing*** by Chris Merchant.

This book may provide a solid understanding of investment basics and reviews some of the content we provide here. The key is understanding that in this age, we bear the responsibility for our future. We no longer enjoy the career stability that our parents and grandparents did, so we must act proactively from day one in investing and meeting our goals.

2. ***Mastering Bitcoin*** by Andreas Antonopoulos

While a technical book, it can help people gain further insight into cryptography and blockchain technology to the point of not only understanding how to make the most out of Bitcoin but also how to deploy your own blockchain. This book is also accessible on the author's Github account. There's a Mastering Ethereum book that complements it if you wish to develop with Ethereum and be part of the web3 community.

3. ***Investing in Ethereum*** by Oscar Flint

This book is more focused on the investing side of Ethereum, and its interrelation with Bitcoin, while also focusing on investment pitfalls.

*4. **Playing with FIRE** by Scott Riekens*

Including a documentary film, this book gives insight into financial freedom and early retirement, while keeping lifestyle and happiness at the center of any retirement endeavor.

*5. **Stablecoin Economy** by Alize Sam, Koosha Azim, and Adam Alonzi.*

This book helps investors make the most of stablecoins amidst an ever-changing crypto and fiat money environment.

Websites

1. **Satoshi Nakamoto Institute** (https://nakamotoinstitute.org)

This website contains Bitcoin's first whitepaper, smart contracts whitepapers, and books on the Cypherpunk movement that was behind the development of Bitcoin's blockchain and the Ethereum Virtual Machine. It's a good website to get insight into the mentality that gave rise to this innovative technology.

2. **CoinCap** (https://coincap.io/)

A website that includes the cryptocurrency market cap for each coin. It's a good starting point for assessing a diversification strategy considering cryptocurrencies.

3. **Bitcoin Project** (https://bitcoin.org/)

This site includes all relevant information about the Bitcoin blockchain, including a comprehensive frequently asked questions guide for inquirers.

4. **Ethereum** (https://ethereum.org/en/)

This site contains all relevant information about the Ethereum Virtual Machine, and introductory guides for smart contracts, stablecoins, and dApps.

5. Iota (https://www.iota.org/)

This is the website for Iota, the developing DAG currency for Internet of Things operations. It might be worth keeping an eye on them and keeping a small part of your portfolio (below 1%) to test it out.

6. Hashgraph (https://hedera.com/)

Hedera is a cryptocurrency using a variation of the DAG structure called the HashGraph. All members have a part of the ledger, but validations are done by a gossip consensus mechanism which is revalidated with delegated proof-of-work.

7. MakerDAO (https://makerdao.com/en/)

This is the official website for the dApp behind DAI, the decentralized crypto-backed stablecoin pegged to the dollar.

8. CityDAO (https://www.citydao.io/)

This is a DAO that gives citizenship rights to its stakeholders, and purchases land by tokenizing it into an NFT.

9. Open Sea (https://opensea.io/)

This website has an NFT catalog with digital artworks.

10. Web3 Foundation (https://web3.foundation/about/)

This site contains all relevant information for Web3 projects.

11. Polkadot (https://polkadot.network/)

Polkadot enables technology for communication between and within blockchains.

Other Resources

1. **Trality Bot Trader** (https://www.trality.com/marketplace)

It's a robo advisor with cryptocurrency investment strategies.

2. **CoinArbitrageBot** (https://coinarbitragebot.com/arbitrage.php)

It's a bot that analyzes BTC value at different exchanges to obtain a margin on arbitrage.

3. **Arbismart** (https://arbismart.com/)

An exchange with its own DAO token offering arbitration services.

4. **Minds** (https://www.minds.com/)

An open-source social network with an ERC-20 token economy based on Ethereum's blockchain technology.

5. **eToro** (https://www.etoro.com/)

A multi-purpose exchange platform including classic assets and cryptocurrencies.

6. **Halving clock** (https://buybitcoinworldwide.com/halving/)

It's a clock with the estimated time of arrival of Bitcoin's next halving   event.

References

Adrian, T., Iyer, T., & Qureshi, M. S. (2022, January 11). *Crypto Prices Move More in Sync With Stocks, Posing New Risks.* IMF. https://www.imf.org/en/Blogs/Articles/2022/01/11/crypto-prices-move-more-in-sync-with-stocks-posing-new-risks

Afolabi, O. (2023, February 27). *What Is Cryptocurrency Compliance, and Why Does It Matter?* MUO. https://www.makeuseof.com/what-is-cryptocurrency-compliance/

Albert, K. (2019, February 7). *The Top 10 Most Informative Books On The FIRE Movement.* GoodPointGrandma. https://goodpointgrandma.com/top-books-fire-movement/

Anspach, D. (2022, December 21). *The Difference Between Pre-Tax and After-Tax Investment Accounts.* The Balance. https://www.thebalancemoney.com/pre-tax-vs-after-tax-investments-what-s-this-mean-2388974

Antonopoulos, A. M. (2018). *Mastering Bitcoin: Programming the Open Blockchain* (2nd ed.). O'Reilly.

Azim, K., Sam, A., & Alonzi, A. (2020). *Stablecoin Economy: Ultimate Guide to Secure Digital Finance.* Koosha Azim.

Baggetta, M. (2019, July 8). *How To Invest in Cryptocurrencies: The Ultimate Beginners Guide.* Blockgeeks. https://blockgeeks.com/guides/how-to-invest-in-cryptocurrencies/

Bahney, A. (2022, May 2). *Here's how to retire long before your 60s.* CNN Business. https://edition.cnn.com/2022/05/02/business/money/how-to-reach-financial-independence-retire-early-fire/index.html

Baltrusaitis, J. (2020, January 28). *Top 15 Must Read Investment Books*. Finbold. https://finbold.com/guide/investment-books/

Banton, C. (2021, July 22). *What is a Bitcoin Whale?* Investopedia. https://www.investopedia.com/terms/b/bitcoin-whale.asp

Benson, A., & Lam-Balfour, T. (2023, January 5). *Investment Strategies for New Investors*. NerdWallet. https://www.nerdwallet.com/article/investing/investment-strategies

Bitcoin. (n.d.). *FAQ*. Bitcoin.org. Retrieved March 5, 2023, from https://bitcoin.org/en/faq#could-users-collude-against-bitcoin

BJM Editorial Team. (2022, November 28). *Best Bitcoin Books for 2023 (with Reader Ratings)*. Bitcoin Market Journal. https://www.bitcoinmarketjournal.com/best-bitcoin-books/

Bloomberg Tax. (2022, August 17). *Analysis of Cryptocurrency Taxation Regulations & Guidelines*. Bloomberg Tax. https://pro.bloombergtax.com/brief/cryptocurrency-taxation-regulations/

Bovaird, C. (2017, July 28). *How to Use Stop Losses in Bitcoin Investing*. Bitcoin Market Journal. https://www.bitcoinmarketjournal.com/bitcoin-stop-loss/

Bradfield, D. (2019, February 13). *Long vs Short Positions in Forex Trading*. DailyFX. https://www.dailyfx.com/education/beginner/long-vs-short-positions-in-forex-trading.html

Burnette, M. (2023, February 17). *Emergency Fund: What it Is and Why it Matters*. NerdWallet. https://www.nerdwallet.com/article/banking/emergency-fund-why-it-matters

Buy Bitcoin Worldwide. (n.d.). *Bitcoin Halving Clock.* Buybitcoinworldwide.com. Retrieved March 2, 2023, from https://buybitcoinworldwide.com/halving/

Buy Bitcoin Worldwide. (2023, February 22). *Bitcoin Price History Chart (Since 2009).* Buybitcoinworldwide.com. https://buybitcoinworldwide.com/price/

Bycko, K. (2021, January 5). *BIP 2021: BITCOIN'S PATH TOWARD RESERVE CURRENCY STATUS IS SET.* Bitcoin Magazine.https://bitcoinmagazine.com/culture/bip-2021-bitcoins-path-toward-reserve-currency-status-is-set

Campos, M. (2022, October 12). *How Much of Your Portfolio Should be in Crypto?* Betterment. https://www.betterment.com/resources/how-much-to-invest-in-crypto

Cech, J. (2022). *A Deep Dive Into IOTA.* CoinMarketCap Alexandria. https://coinmarketcap.com/alexandria/article/a-deep-dive-into-iota

CFI Team. (2023, January 13). *Compound Interest.* Corporate Finance Institute. https://corporatefinanceinstitute.com/resources/wealth-management/compound-interest/

ChoiseCom. (2023, February 22). *The Bitcoin market cycles: what you need to know 2023.* CoinMarketCap. https://coinmarketcap.com/community/articles/63f644360f58c754df eed6af/

Chow, A. (2021, March 22). *NFTs Are Shaking Up the Art World—But They Could Change So Much More.* Time. https://time.com/5947720/nft-art/

Coehlo-Prahbu, S. (2020, January 6). A *Beginner's Guide to Decentralized Finance (DeFi)*. https://www.coinbase.com/blog/a-beginners-guide-to-decentralized-finance-defi

Coin Insider. (2021, July 9). *Risk Management in Crypto Trading: Simple Rules to Follow*. Coin Insider. https://www.coininsider.com/risk-management-in-crypto-trading/

Coindesk. (n.d.). *What is staking?* Coinbase.com. Retrieved February 26, 2023, from https://www.coinbase.com/es/learn/crypto-basics/what-is-staking

Cote, C. (2021, September 28). *How to Diversify Your Portfolio with Alternative Investments*. Business Insights Blog. https://online.hbs.edu/blog/post/how-to-diversify-your-portfolio

Cryptonews. (2022). *How To Store Cryptocurrency Safely in 2022*. Cryptonews.com. https://cryptonews.com/guides/how-to-store-cryptocurrency-safely.htm

dcaBTC. (n.d.). *Dollar Cost Averaging Bitcoin*. Dcabtc.com. Retrieved February 26, 2023, from https://dcabtc.com/

Dealbreuin, J. (2021, August 21). *15 Good Reasons To Retire Early*. Financial Freedom Countdown. https://financialfreedomcountdown.com/reasons-to-retire-early/

Dixon, A. (2018, September 12). *5 Factors to Consider When Rebalancing Your Portfolio*. SmartAsset. https://smartasset.com/investing/factors-to-consider-when-rebalancing-your-portfolio

Edelman, G. (2021, November 29). *What Is Web3, Anyway?* Wired. https://www.wired.com/story/web3-gavin-wood-interview/

Egede, I. (2022, January 28). *How to Sell Cryptocurrency*. InsideBitcoins.com. https://insidebitcoins.com/sell-cryptocurrency

Ethereum. (n.d.). *Decentralized finance (DeFi)*. Ethereum.org. Retrieved February 27, 2023, from https://ethereum.org/en/defi/

Ethereum. (2023, January 19). *Ethereum Virtual Machine (EVM)*. Ethereum.org. https://ethereum.org/en/developers/docs/evm/

Evans, T. (2019, April 1). *A long-term disciplined investment approach*. Progeny. https://theprogenygroup.com/blog/long-term-disciplined-investment-approach/

Fernando, J. (2022, December 1). *Arbitrage: How Arbitraging Works in Investing, With Examples*. Investopedia. https://www.investopedia.com/terms/a/arbitrage.asp

Fidelity. (2015). *What Is Portfolio Diversification?* Fidelity.com. https://www.fidelity.com/learning-center/investment-products/mutual-funds/diversification

Fries, T. (2023, January 9). *Complete Guide to Market Cycles*. Tokenist. https://tokenist.com/investing/market-cycle/

Gaines, K. (2020, January 21). *18 Risks You Face In Retirement*. American Financial Management Group | Philadelphia Financial Planner. https://afmgplanning.com/18-risks-you-face-in-retirement/

Gatsby, J. (2022, September 2). *Beyond Democracy: The Network City*. Welcometowonderland.substack.com. https://welcometowonderland.substack.com/p/beyond-democracy-the-network-city

Geier, B. (2023, January 7). *10 Types of Investments (and How They Work)*. SmartAsset. https://smartasset.com/investing/types-of-investment

George, B. (2022, April 27). *What Are PFP NFTs?* Coindesk. https://www.coindesk.com/learn/what-are-pfp-nfts/

Gobler, E. (2022, June 26). *Why You Should Start Investing When You're Young*. The Balance. https://www.thebalancemoney.com/the-advantages-of-investing-in-your-20s-5179604

Gravier, E. (2022, April 7). *Here are the 7 biggest investing mistakes you want to avoid, according to financial experts*. CNBC. https://www.cnbc.com/select/biggest-investing-mistakes/

Grohol, J. M., Styles, K., & Craft, C. (2022, March 31). *FOMO: Causes and Solutions*. Psych Central. https://psychcentral.com/health/what-is-fomo-the-fear-of-missing-out#recap

Hartill, R. (2020, October 21). *This Is Why FIRE Is a Wildly Unrealistic Retirement Strategy for Most People*. The Motley Fool. https://www.fool.com/investing/2020/10/21/this-is-why-fire-is-a-wildly-unrealistic-retiremen/

Hayes, A. (2019). *Inside the Risk/Reward Ratio*. Investopedia. https://www.investopedia.com/terms/r/riskrewardratio.asp

Hedera. (n.d.). *What is hashgraph consensus?* Hedera. Retrieved March 5, 2023, from https://hedera.com/learning/hedera-hashgraph/what-is-hashgraph-consensus

Hunt, D. (2022, January 7). *Why Having a Goal Is Key to Investing*. Morgan Stanley. https://www.morganstanley.com/access/investing-goals/

IBM. (2022). *What are smart contracts on blockchain?* IBM. https://www.ibm.com/topics/smart-contracts

Jennings, M. (2022, April 7). *Decentralization for Web3 Builders: Principles, Models, How*. A16z Crypto. https://a16zcrypto.com/content/article/web3-decentralization-models-framework-principles-how-to/

Kastrenakes, J. (2021, March 11). *Beeple sold an NFT for $69 million.* The Verge. https://www.theverge.com/2021/3/11/22325054/beeple-christies-nft-sale-cost-everydays-69-million

Klimashousky, D. (2019, July 23). *Making an Investment Plan: A Step-by-Step Guide.* SmartAsset. https://smartasset.com/investing/how-to-make-an-investment-plan

Kozak, S., & Gajdek, S. (2021). Risk of Investment in Cryptocurrencies. *Economic and Regional Studies / Studia Ekonomiczne I Regionalne, 14*(3), 294–304. https://doi.org/10.2478/ers-2021-0021

Küllmer, F. K. (2022, December 12). *Where Is the Ethereum Virtual Machine Headed in 2023? (Hint: Beyond Ethereum).* Www.coindesk.com. https://www.coindesk.com/consensus-magazine/2022/12/12/ethereum-virtual-machine-evm-future/

Lacey, B. (2020, May 10). *10 Smart Strategies to Achieve Financial Independence.* The Scope of Practice. https://www.thescopeofpractice.com/10-smart-strategies-to-achieve-financial-independence/

Lemire, K. A. (2022, September 26). *Cryptocurrency and anti-money laundering enforcement.* Reuters. https://www.reuters.com/legal/transactional/cryptocurrency-anti-money-laundering-enforcement-2022-09-26/

Likos, P. (2021, May 21). *What Are Stablecoins and How Can I Invest in Them?* US News. https://money.usnews.com/investing/cryptocurrency/articles/what-are-stablecoins-and-how-can-i-invest-in-them

Makarov, I., & Schoar, A. (2021). *Blockchain Analysis of the Bitcoin Market.* https://doi.org/10.3386/w29396

MakerDAO. (n.d.). *Maker - Whitepaper.* Makerdao.com. Retrieved March 6, 2023, from https://makerdao.com/en/whitepaper/

Marcobello, M. (2022, June 29). *What Are Layer 2s and Why Are They Important?* Coin Desk. https://www.coindesk.com/learn/what-are-layer-2s-and-why-are-they-important/

Marquit, M. (2022, December 23). *What Is the FIRE Movement and Is It for You?* Britannica Money. https://www.britannica.com/money/financial-independence-retire-early

May, T. C. (1992, September 1). *Libertaria in Cyberspace.* Satoshi Nakamoto Institute. https://nakamotoinstitute.org/libertaria-in-cyberspace/

Meta, S. (n.d.). *Cryptocurrency Trading: Buy-and-Hold Strategy for Crypto Trading.* FX Leaders. Retrieved February 26, 2023, from https://www.fxleaders.com/learn-crypto/strategies/the-buy-and-hold-approach/

Minds. (n.d.). *Whitepaper.* Retrieved March 8, 2023, from https://www.minds.com/static/en/assets/documents/Whitepaper-v0.5.pdf

Musharraf, M. (2022, October 25). *What is the Blockchain Trilemma?* Ledger. https://www.ledger.com/academy/what-is-the-blockchain-trilemma

Nakamoto, S. (2008, October 8). *Bitcoin: a Peer-to-Peer Electronic Cash System.* Satoshi Nakamoto Institute. https://nakamotoinstitute.org/bitcoin/

Narain, A., & Moretti, M. (2022, September). *Regulating Crypto.* IMF. https://www.imf.org/en/Publications/fandd/issues/2022/09/Regulating-crypto-Narain-Moretti

Ng, J. (2023, January 1). *5 Modern Asset Portfolio Allocation Models & Strategies.* Dollarbureau.com. https://dollarbureau.com/blog/asset-portfolio-allocation-models/

O'Neill, J., Hussey, M., & Chipolina, S. (2022, April 29). *What Are Decentralized Applications (Dapps)?* Decrypt. https://decrypt.co/resources/what-are-decentralized-applications-dapps

Open Sea. (n.d.). *What are NFT drops?* Open Sea. Retrieved March 6, 2023, from https://opensea.io/learn/what-are-nft-drops

Palmer, B. (2023, February 26). *5 Tips for Diversifying Your Portfolio.* Investopedia. https://www.investopedia.com/articles/03/072303.asp

Perez, K. (2020, March 27). *Investment Trackers: Ways to Monitor Your Portfolio.* Investor Junkie. https://investorjunkie.com/investing/how-to-track-your-investments/

Phemex. (2021, June 2). *Momentum Trading: Crypto momentum trading Strategies.* Phemex Academy. https://phemex.com/academy/bitcoin-momentum-trading

Principal. (2023, February 10). *5 reasons why investing young makes a big difference later on.* Principal.com. https://www.principal.com/individuals/build-your-knowledge/reasons-why-investing-makes-a-big-difference-later-on

Putzhammer, M. (2022, August 19). *How to Diversify Your Crypto Portfolio and Limit Risk.* Trality Blog. https://www.trality.com/blog/diversify-your-crypto-portfolio

Putzhammer, M. (2023, February 1). *The Ultimate Guide to Copy Trading Crypto (2023).* Trality Blog. https://www.trality.com/blog/copy-trading-guide

PwC. (2022). *PwC Global Crypto Regulation Report 2023.* https://www.pwc.com/gx/en/new-ventures/cryptocurrency-assets/pwc-global-crypto-regulation-report-2023.pdf

Ramsey Solutions. (2022, September 30). *What Is the F.I.R.E. Movement?* Ramsey Solutions. https://www.ramseysolutions.com/retirement/what-is-the-fire-movement

Rebane, C. (2018, August 15). *11 Best Books on Ethereum – Must Read!* Cryptalker. https://cryptalker.com/11-best-books-on-ethereum/

Reuters. (2021, May 13). *Factbox: How big is Bitcoin's carbon footprint?* Reuters. https://www.reuters.com/technology/how-big-is-bitcoins-carbon-footprint-2021-05-13/

Rigiglioso, M. (2007, October 1). Research: *How the Fear of Missing Out Makes Investors Risk Blind.* Stanford Graduate School of Business. https://www.gsb.stanford.edu/insights/research-how-fear-missing-out-makes-investors-risk-blind

Rosen, A. (2023, February 14). *What is cryptocurrency? A Guide For Beginners.* NerdWallet. https://www.nerdwallet.com/article/investing/cryptocurrency

Rosen, A., & Woock, K. (2022, September 12). *How to Buy Cryptocurrency: What Investors Should Know.* NerdWallet.

https://www.nerdwallet.com/article/investing/how-to-buy-cryptocurrency

Royal, J. (2022, November 23). *How To Start Investing In Cryptocurrency: A Guide For Beginners.* Bankrate. https://www.bankrate.com/investing/how-to-invest-in-cryptocurrency-beginners-guide/

Ruane, J., & McAfee, A. (2022, May 10). *What a DAO Can — and Can't — Do.* Harvard Business Review. https://hbr.org/2022/05/what-a-dao-can-and-cant-do

Rueffer, S. (n.d.). *How to Become a Profitable Trader in 8 Simple Steps.* TradingXplained. Retrieved March 6, 2023, from http://tradingxplained.com/stock-trading-101/how-to-become-a-profitable-trader-in-8-simple-steps/

Schwab, C. (n.d.-a). *Cryptocurrency Investing.* Schwab Brokerage. Retrieved March 1, 2023, from https://www.schwab.com/cryptocurrency

Schwab, C. (n.d.-b). *Investing Principles. Schwab Brokerage.* Retrieved March 5, 2023, from https://www.schwab.com/investing-principles

Schwab, C. (n.d.-c). *What Should Your Retirement Portfolio Include?* Schwab Brokerage. Retrieved February 24, 2023, from https://www.schwab.com/retirement-portfolio

Sergeenkov, A. (2021a, November 4). *Crypto Arbitrage Trading: How to Make Low-Risk Gains.* Coin Desk. https://www.coindesk.com/learn/crypto-arbitrage-trading-how-to-make-low-risk-gains/

Sergeenkov, A. (2021b, November 29). *What Is Cryptocurrency?* Coin Desk. https://www.coindesk.com/learn/what-is-cryptocurrency/

Sergeenkov, A. (2023, January 13). *What Is an Automated Market Maker?* Coin Desk. https://www.coindesk.com/learn/what-is-an-automated-market-maker/

Sharkey, S. (2022, July 18). *How To Avoid Lifestyle Inflation: 9 Key Ways.* Clever Girl Finance. https://www.clevergirlfinance.com/blog/lifestyle-inflation/

SoFi. (2020, September 10). *6 Investment Risk Management Strategies.* SoFi. https://www.sofi.com/learn/content/investment-risk-management/

Spurrier, H. (2021, January 14). *8 Good Financial Habits You Need to Adopt Immediately.* Savology. https://savology.com/good-financial-habits

Stackpole, T. (2022, May 10). *What Is Web3?* Harvard Business Review. https://hbr.org/2022/05/what-is-web3

Swenson, S. (2022, November 30). *How to Set Investment Goals.* The Motley Fool. https://www.fool.com/investing/how-to-invest/how-to-set-investment-goals/

Szabo, N. (1996). *Credit With Privity.* Satoshi Nakamoto Institute. https://nakamotoinstitute.org/credit-with-privity/

The Family Office. (2022, May 29). *Risk Mitigation: How to Minimize Risk in your Investment Portfolio.* Tfoco.com. https://www.tfoco.com/en/insights/articles/risk-mitigation-explained

Valkenburgh, P. V. (2017, October 17). *What is "open source" and why is it important?* Coin Center. https://www.coincenter.org/education/advanced-topics/open-source/

Wallstreetmojo Team. (2022, June 23). *Asset Allocation.* WallStreetMojo. https://www.wallstreetmojo.com/asset-allocation/

Web3 Foundation. (n.d.). *About.* Web3 Foundation. Retrieved March 7, 2023, from https://web3.foundation/about/

White, K., Goel, A., & Waliczek, S. (2022, March 28). *What is the current state of cryptocurrency regulation?* World Economic Forum. https://www.weforum.org/agenda/2022/03/where-is-cryptocurrency-regulation-heading/

White, K., Waliscek, S., & Mandeng, O. (2022, July 20). *Here's what you need to know about cryptocurrency regulation.* World Economic Forum. https://www.weforum.org/agenda/2022/07/cryptocurrency-regulation-global-standard/

Wood, G. (2016). *POLKADOT: VISION FOR A HETEROGENEOUS MULTI-CHAIN FRAMEWORK DRAFT 1.* In Polkadot. https://assets.polkadot.network/Polkadot-whitepaper.pdf

Zaghw, I. (2022, December 22). *Investment Risk Profile Examples: 5 Main Risk Profiles Explained.* FinMasters. https://finmasters.com/investment-risk-profile-examples/

Zetzsche, D. A., Arner, D. W., & Buckley, R. P. (2020). Decentralized Finance. *Journal of Financial Regulation*, 6(2), 172–203. https://doi.org/10.1093/jfr/fjaa010

www.ingramcontent.com/pod-product-compliance
Lightning Source LLC
Chambersburg PA
CBHW070613220526
45467CB00003B/1412